DAYS PLEASANT AND UNPLEASANT

DAYS PLEASANT AND UNPLEASANT

IN THE ORDER

SONS OF ITALY IN AMERICA

THE PROBLEM OF RACES AND RACIAL SOCIETIES
IN THE UNITED STATES

ASSIMILATION OR ISOLATION

BY

ROBERT FERRARI

[1926]

WITH A NEW FOREWORD BY
FRANCESCO CORDASCO

AUGUSTUS M. KELLEY • PUBLISHERS
CLIFTON 1974

First Edition 1926

(*New York* : Mandy Press, 1926)

Reprinted 1974 by

Augustus M. Kelley Publishers

Clifton New Jersey 07012

Library of Congress Cataloging in Publication Data

```
Ferrari, Robert.
   Days pleasant and unpleasant in the Order Sons of
Italy in America.

   Reprint of the ed. published by Mandy Press,
New York.
   1.  Order of Sons of Italy in America.  2.  Italians
in the United States.  I.  Title.
HS1848.06F47  1973          301.45'15'1073        73-13551
ISBN 0-678-01363-2
```


PRINTED IN THE UNITED STATES OF AMERICA
by SENTRY PRESS, NEW YORK, N. Y. 10013
Bound by A. HOROWITZ & SON, CLIFTON, N. J.

FOREWORD

One of the major tasks facing American academicians studying the experiences of ethnic groups in the United States is the collection of the primary source materials out of which an ethnic socio-historiography may be fashioned: at best, it is a difficult task, not only because of the scarcity (if not, unavailability) of the materials. The study of the Italian experience in the United States particularly underscores the formidability of the task, and all of its attendant problems.

Since the late 1960s (and concomitant with the new interest in ethnicity, itself deriving from the civil rights movements of the last two decades and the new Black consciousness which accompanied it), I have undertaken the assembly of a corpus of works which delineated the Italian American experience. Initially, I concentrated on earlier important scholarly works, out of print and generally unobtainable;[1] but the greater need lay elsewhere. As I noted in my *Italians in the United States: A Bibliography.* . . . "Beyond the handful of early scholarly studies, there is a large primary source material which deals with the life of the Italian community in American: more often than not, these primary sources are the observations of Italian immigrants; an improvised and tendentious literature which appears under a rich mosaic of imprints, it is the very substance of the recorded life of the Italian subcommunity and, in this sense, invaluable to the new American historio-

---

[1] I edited the unpublished doctoral dissertation (1944) of Leonard Covello, *The Social Background of the Italo-American School Child: A Study of the Southern Italian Mores and Their Effect on the School Situation in Italy and America* (Leiden, The Netherlands: E.J. Brill, 1967; Totowa, N. J. : Rowman & Littlefield, 1972); and I have prepared forewords/introductions to the following works which have been reissued: Robert F. Foerster, *The Italian Emigration of Our Time* (New York: Russell & Russell, 1968; originally, Harvard University Press, 1919); Phyllis H. Williams, *South Italian Folkways in Europe and America: A Handbook for Social Workers, Visiting Nurses, School Teachers and Physicians* (New York: Russell & Russell, 1969; originally, Yale University Press, 1938); Irvin L. Child, *Italian or American?: The Second Generation in Conflict* (New York: Russell & Russell, 1970; originally Yale University Press, 1943); Joseph W. Tait, *Some Aspects of the Effects of the Dominant American Culture Upon Children of Italian-Born Parents* (Clifton, N. J. : Augustus M. Kelley, 1972; originally, Teachers College, Columbia University, 1942); *Vito Marcantonio: Selected Debates, Speeches, and Writings* (Clifton, N. J. : Augustus M. Kelley, 1973; orginially, Vito Marcantonio Memorial, 1956).

graphy."[2] It is to this category that Robert Ferrari's *Days Pleasant and Un-
Pleasant* belongs. It is part of that *ephemera* churned out of the "round-of-
life" of the Italian subcommunity; and its rarity (typical of the tract of its
genre) is due to the short-run issue of the tract by a job printer turned
publisher.[3]

What is remarkable about *Days Pleasant and Unpleasant* is Robert Ferrari's attempt (however inadriotly) to orchestrate the history of his quarrels in the *Sons of Italy* into a mock literary form; and so, he provides a
dramatis personae, and casts the main characters in poetic apostrophes. The
quarrel, at best, is less important than the insights which Ferrari's tract
provides into the workings of the *Order Sons of Italy in America,*[4] and
more directly into what Ferrari calls "the problem of races and racial societies in the United States: assimilation or isolation?" Ferrari was convinced
that the *Order Sons of Italy* was inimical to the best interests of Italians in
the United States. His opposition to the *Order* transcended the schismatic
quarrel in which he was involved (the essence of the separatist struggle is re-
capitulated on pp. 92-94); what Ferrari was reacting to was the *Order's* in-
ability to come together as a cohesive force in the Italian community, and
thereby to achieve political power, essentially what he called "The solidification and the unification of the Italian strength in the United States."

It was discord that Ferrari deplored, and his perceptive recognition that,
in the absence of a united strength, the needs of the Italian community

---

[2] F. Cordasco, *Italians in the United States: A Bibliography of Reports, Texts,
Critical Studies and Related Materials* (New York: Oriole Editions, 1972), p. xiv.
Thus far, beyond the present work (in this critical area of primary materials), I have
prepared forewords for the following which have been reissued: Antonio Mangano,
Sons of Italy: A Social and Religious Study of the Italians in America (New York:
Russell & Russell 1972; originally, Missionary Education Movement of the United
States and Canada, 1917): Enrico C. Sartorio, *Social and Religious Life of Italians in
America* (Clifton, N.J.: Augustus M. Kelley, 1973; originally, Christopher Publishing
House, 1918).

[3] Robert Ferrari, *Days Pleasant and Unpleasant in the Order Sons of Italy in Ameri-
ca: The Problem of Races and Racial Societies in the United States. Assimilation or
Isolation? Giorni Di Piacere e Disgusto Passati Nell'Ordine Figli D'Italia in America
Dal Maggio 1925 al Febbraio 1926* (New York: Mandy Press, 1926).

[4] The history of the *Order* is still to be written (in 1917, Mangano [*op. cit.,* p. 129]
notes that the order [founded in 1905 in New York] comprised 623 lodges in twenty
states, with a membership of 80,000; by 1926, Ferrari estimated the membership at
300,000.) See generally, Ernest L. Biagi, *The Purple Aster: A History of the Order
Sons of Italy in America* (New York: Veritas Publishing Co., 1961); and Baldo Aquilano, *L'Ordine Figli d'Italia in America . . .* (New York: Società Tipografica Italiana,
1925).

ii

were not being met. In his words:

> The Italians should be ashamed of themselves. From over
> three millions of Italians in the United States and over a million
> of Italians in the City of New York, it is difficult to get any
> harmony or concord of action in any useful or noble purpose.
> There are thousands of institutions necessary for the Italians
> but these institutions are not erected. There is too much desire
> of individuals to become prominent and there is too much per-
> sonality. There is no submersion of the individual in the com-
> mon good as there is in the case of other races in the United
> States. The Jews are just now in a campaign for the raising of
> fifteen million dollars, six million of which has to be raised in
> the City of New York. Within a very short time that fifteen
> millions will be raised. What could not the Italians do with
> $1,000,000. And yet, even if they were able to gather together
> one million dollars, there would be so much squabbling among
> the leaders and directors, that harmony of action would be par-
> alyzed and nothing would be done with the money. (p. 90)[5]

It was a prophetic statement. Italians were never to achieve the unity
which Ferrari sought, and the reasons lay in a complex constellation of
forces in which village-mindedness or provincialism *(Companilismo)* was
the dominating determinant. It is too early to assess the new ethnic consciousness manifested by Italian Americans in the present period (what
Nicholas Pileggi has called "Risorgimento: the Red, White, and Greening

---

[5] Ferrari's comparative notice of the Jewish community has a special significance.
"The 'Little Italies' scattered over America prior to 1881, had formed no central social
organizations likely to contend with political or social problems. Nor had any social
establishment been created which might serve as a model for the new immigrant in
his efforts to rise to a higher class. In contrast to this, American Israel even before
1881 had established national organizations like the Board of Delegates, regional phi-
lantropic organizations as well as a social establishment. This establishment consisted
of a merchant class dispersed over the whole of America, but concentrated in the
largest cities." Rudolf Glanz, *Jew and Italian: Historic Group Relations and the New
Immigration, 1881-1924* (New York: Ktav Publishing Co., 1971), p. 10.

[6] For *Campanilismo,* see Covello, *op. cit.;* and, with caution, Nathan Glazer and
Daniel P. Moyihan, *Beyond the Melting Pot: The Negroes, Puerto Ricans, Jews, Italians,
and Irish of New York City* (Cambridge: M.I.T. Press, 1963/1970). Child, *op. cit.,* has
continuing value in this matter; and reference should be made to Herbert J. Gans, *The
Urban Villagers: Group and Class in the Life of Italian Americans* (New York: Free
Press, 1962). It is not inappropriate to repeat (of the non-Italian participant observers)
the caution as expressed in my introduction to the Child reprint: "The demos of the
Italian community eludes Gans, overwhelms Glazer, and at times escapes Child. All
three men suffered in different degrees the disadvantages of outsiders studying a community. In a word, they were not Italians."

of New York");[7] but there is some truth in Erik Amfitheatrof's observation: "Clearly, many Italian-Americans are today responding to the complicated forces loosed by their assimilation into the American mainstream. The children of Italian immigrants no longer feel Italian. They are American. In shedding a sense of apartness from American life, they have also relinquished their once-powerful emotional associations with a remote Italian world that they knew secondhand, from family recollections and legends. A void has been created, and they are now beginning to reevaluate their ethnic past—which is Italian-American rather than Italian—because it is an inescapable part of what they think about themselves, and what they tell their children."[8]

Of course, Ferrari never intrudes into those areas of race/nationality which were tragically explored by Gino Speranza and which led to a repudiation of his Italianate identity;[9] and Ferrari lies totally outside the intricate investigations of sociologists and psychologists who have attempted to discern the complicated dynamics of conflict and acculturation amongst Italian-Americans. But this does not diminsh the importance of Ferrari's tract; on the contrary, Ferrari helps explain the alienation of Speranza (and of untold numbers of others), and he affords insights which are absent in the socio-psychological portraits of outside participant-observors.

There is little personal information available about Ferrari. My friend and colleague, Leonard Covello, who knew Ferrari, describes him as "an intense intellectual, certainly rare in the Italian community, with an integrity of purpose and commitment to Italian needs, and a man shabbily

---

[7] Nicholas Pileggi, "The Risorgimento of Italian Power: The Red, White and Greening of New York," *New York,* vol. 4 (June 7, 1971); see also, Richard Gambino, "Twenty Million Italians Can't Be Wrong." *New York Times* (April 30, 1972) which is somewhat superficial, but itself a manifestation of the resurgence of *Italianita.* An excellent discussion of the new Italian consciousness is in Silvano M. Tomasi, *The Italians in America* (New York: Istituto Italiana di Cultura, Occasional Paper. July 1971).

[8] Erik Amfitheatrof, *The Children of Columbus: An Informal History of the Italians in the New World* (Boston: Little Brown and Co., 1973); p. 324. For a notice of Amfitheatrof and other recent works, see F. Cordasco, "The Children of Columbus: Recent Works on the Italian American Experience," *Contemporary Sociology: A Journal of Reviews,* vol. 2 (November, 1973).

[9] See Gino C. Speranza, *Race or Nationality: A Conflict of Divided Loyalties* (Indianapolis: Bobbs Merrill, 1920. Speranza (1872-1927), who was Secretary of the Society for the Protection of Italian Immigrants, is a neglected figure who deserves a full scale study; his letters and papers are deposited in the New York Public Library. An incomplete but representative list of his writings is in F. Cordasco, *Italians in the United States: A Bibliography . . . .* As a contrast to Speranza's views expressed in *Race or Nationality,* see his earlier writings on assimilation, *e.g.,* "How it Feels to be a Problem: A Consideration of Certain Causes which prevent or retard Assimilation," *Charities,* vol. 12 (May 7, 1904), pp. 457-463.

treated by his kinsmen less able than he. " Certainly, the characterization
rings true. There is a tragic awareness in Ferrari's questions posed to fellow
Italians almost a half-century ago, and a poignant eloquence as well:

> What is the present position of the Italian group in this coun-
> try in relation to other groups? What ought its position to be
> with respect to other groups? What contribution should be
> made to American life by the Italian group? How should that
> contribution be made? Should the Italian group and other
> groups be allowed absolute and unfettered freedom to develop,
> and make their contribution, or should they be cribbed, cabined,
> and confined by restrictions placed upon them by the American
> government, or by any group, racial or economic in this coun-
> try . . . . The hope of the American of the future lies in the
> fostering and the cherishing of the American born of foreign
> descent because he is the reflection of the environment in
> which he lives and in which he has been brought up; and this
> environment is the American scene.

All of which has particular significance at our moment in time.

FRANCESCO CORDASCO
Montclair State College

DAYS PLEASANT AND UNPLEASANT

in the

ORDER SONS OF ITALY IN AMERICA

—

The Problem of Races and Racial Societies
in the United States

—

ASSIMILATION OR ISOLATION?

by

ROBERT FERRARI

GIORNI DI PIACERE E DISGUSTO

passati nell'Ordine Figli d'Italia in America
dal Maggio 1925 al Febbraio 1926

di

ROBERT FERRARI

PREFACE

Debate is interesting in itself. It is even more interesting when great principles are involved. Assimilation or isolation of foreign groups in this country is the most pressing as it is the perennial and permanent question in our life till the question is decided right.

This small book seeks to answer that question in the interest of the present and the future of the life of this country — a present and a future inexricably bound up with the proper solution of the problem of races here and their relations one with another.

But the reader will find no abstract discussion. We have had too many airy discussions without a local habitation and a name. The conclusion here is short, concrete and vivid; and the reasoning upon which it is based is founded upon actual life lived and actual events occurred. The facts I have been confronted with in my experience as an officer of the largest society of Italians in the United States. It is said there are in the Order Sons of Italy 300,000 members. There are 3,000,000 Italians in the United States. Directly or indirectly then, the Order touches almost every one of Italian birth or descent in America. It is therefore advisable to begin an open discussion of the effects of this Order and similar Orders and Societies in the United States and study how they affect the Societies themselves, the members individually and how these individuals and Societies affect the American body politic. My conclusion is adverse to the Societies as retarding and preventing assimilation with Americans.

The grave danger is that as during the war the governors of the Nation may make the fatal mistake of forceful imposition of culture and of assimilation; and thus drive the younger generation into the arms of their natural enemies — the anti-assimilationists and isolationists.

The argument is high. My wish is that the treatment may be elevated.

ROBERT FERRARI

TABLE OF CONTENTS

INTRODUCTION

I entered the Order in February 1926, thinking that I could be of service to it and to the Italians in the United States and to this, the land of my birth. I had always kept away from Italian Societies and had lived a life of labor among my fellow Americans of all races.

A division in the Order took place in July 1926. A group, met at a convention in New York. The other group met in Schenectady. I went to Schenectady. I was elected President of the Mortuary Fund—a fund which had reached the sum of $200,000.

Upon our arrival in New York City on August 9th, we began to set up the necessary machinery. Soon difficulties arose between the officers and me. Soon took place the clash of temperaments, traditions, experiences. A series of differences which are detailed in the following pages, led to the crisis meeting of January 12, 1926, when ungentlemanly conduct and unlawful methods brought about the climax of endurance.

I was being pressed to make from the death funds of my Commission a loan to pay attorneys with in a litigation pending between the two groups above mentioned. I refused. Soon after I resigned from the Presidency of the Mortuary Fund, from the position of Counsel to the Grand Lodge of the State of New York and from the Order. My disgust was great.

I thought I should be left in quiet to attend to my own affairs. But I reckoned without my host. My resignation had produced revolution in the ranks: the rank and file wanted to know the reasons for my going. The Order had to satisfy this desire. Two months after my resignation, a Communication from the Mortuary Fund appeared in the Italian papers which was so framed and worded as to say I had left the Order for personal reasons and not for reasons of policy or administration; adding I had signed a check for $2500 with which to make a loan to the Grand Council of our group of the Order, the Grand Council with this loan paying the New York State share of the Attorneys fees. It implied also that I had voted for the loan. I had not.

I replied with an interview given to Ernest Valentini, one of the best journalists in America. The discussion went on for over a month—the officers of my group of the Order making the wildest and most extravagant statements. I was bound first to attend to my professional business and Icould not therefore keep up the running fire in a guerilla warfare in which these men are past masters and for which they have the necessary leisure. Soon the muck was in the air. They are, too, past masters of the art of slinging mud. I decided to reply to all and to set out the facts of my connection with the Order. Hence this book. Hinc illae lacrymae: Hence their tears.

DAYS PLEASANT AND UNPLEASANT

in the

ORDER SONS OF ITALY IN AMERICA

MAY 14, 1925 to FEBRUARY 3, 1926

A COMEDY

Dramatis Personae: Cast of Characters

THE NOBLE BAND:

The Grand Executive Council:

Grand Venerable	J. J. Freschi
Assistant Grand Venerable	G. Rossi
Grand Orator	F. Catinella
Grand Treasurer	P. Provenzano
Grand Recording Secretary	C. Pitocchi
Grand Financial Secretary	G. Galante

Grand Trustees:

A. Angrisani	S. Di Stefano
V. Iannone	U. Miele

G. Stramiello

Mortuary Fund Commission:

President	Robert Ferrari
Treasurer	P. Gallo
Secretary	M. De Pasquale

Commissioners:

A. Aleprando	A. Apollo
N. Calivá	A. Cuomo Cerulli
A. Fagá	C. Le Porte
C. Linfante	P. Miele

V. Capparrelli	Editor Nuovo Vessillo and Grand Delegate
F. Panetta	Acting Grand Recording Secretary

CHARACTERIZATIONS OF THE CAST
and
PREMONITIONS OF THE DRAMA

Grand Council:

The right divine of kings to govern wrong.—Pope.
Now hangs as mute on Tara's walls
As if that soul were fled.—Thomas Moore.

F. U. M.

To found a great empire for the sole purpose of raising up a people of customers is a project fit only for a nation of shopkeepers.—Adapted from Adam Smith.

Fast bind, fast find;

A proverb never stale in thrifty mind.—Shakespeare.

Stephen Miele

False face must hide what the false heart doth know.—Shakespeare.
Who drives fat oxen should himself be fat.—Samuel Johnson.
No creature smarts so little as a fool.—Pope.
**A motley fool.
A worthy fool! Motley's the only wear.—Shakespeare.
A fool's bolt is soon shot.—Shakespeare.
There's no fool like the old one.—Tennyson.
All my fortunes are at sea.—Shakespeare.
As foul,
As Vulcan's stithy.—Shakespeare.
He that is giddy thinks the world turns round.—Shakespeare.
Here we may reign secure; and, in my choice,
To reign is worth ambition though in Hell;
Better to reign in Hell than serve in Heaven.—Milton.
Whatever record leap to light,
He shall never be shamed.—Tennyson.

Panetta

Ingrate, faith-breaker, good-hater.
If that ain't Judas on the largest scale.—Holmes.
The worst of madmen is a saint run mad.—Pope.
A little round, fat, oily man of God.—Thomson.
Deep in yon cave Honorious long did dwell,
In hope to merit Heaven by making earth a hell.—Byron.
Ingratitude, thou marble-hearted fiend,
More hideous ** than the sea monster!—Shakespeare.

Robert Ferrari

Twelfth Night; or what you will.
It's Tommy this, an' Tommy that, an' "Tommy 'ow's yer soul?"
But it's "Thin red line of 'eroes" when the drums begin to
roll.—Kipling.
Homeless near a thousand homes I stood,
And near a thousand tables pined and wanted food.—Words-
worth.
'Tis dangerous to disturb a hornet's nest.—Dryden.

Capparrelli:

Tears, idle tears.—Tennyson.
Then went to bed and slept as sound,
As if I'd paid a note.—Lanier.

The Rest of the Cast: Rubberstamps.

Fools are my theme, let satire be my song.—Byron.

Satire's my weapon, but I'm too discreet
To run amuck, and tilt at all I meet.—Pope.

As idly as a painted ship.
Upon a painted ocean.—Ibid.

Things unattempted yet in prose or rhyme.—Milton.

The tree that bears no fruit deserves no name.—Young.

Happy who in his verse can gently steer,
From grave to light; from pleasant to severe.—Dryden.

Heat not a furnace for your foe so hot
That it do singe yourself.—Shakespeare.

Speak of me as I am; nothing extenuate,
Nor set down aught in malice.—Shakespeare.

My foot is on my native heath, and my name is MacGregor.—
Scott.

Flint shows not till it be struck.—Shakespeare.

He makes no friend who never made a foe.—Tennyson.

History—is indeed, little more than the register of the crimes,
follies and misfortunes of mankind.—Gibbon.

'Tain't a knowing kind o'cattle
Thet is ketched with mouldy corn.—Lowell.

Work Done by Me as Counsel for the Grand Lodge, Order Sons of Italy in America—Schenectady Group, in the Case of the Order Sons of Italy in America Against the Sons of Italy Grand Lodge.

For the first four weeks there were meetings of the Law Committee almost every day, the meetings lasting from three to six hours each time.

My first memorandum was presented on the 12th of August, 1925.

My second memorandum was presented on the 17th of August. This was the memorandum concerning the law and facts of the case.

My third memorandum—my second concerning the law and the facts of the case—was a memorandum of 47 pages and was in first draft presented on August, 25, 1925.

The final draft was completed about September 7, 1925.

In addition to meetings of the law committee and combined meetings of lawyers and laymen in connection with the discussion of the facts and the law of the case against the Sons of Italy Grand Lodge; and in addition to research work and thought on the problems involved in the case and the writing of memoranda and briefs, I advised over the telephone at my office, hundreds of people connected with the subordinate lodges, the F. U. M. and the Grand Council as well as the Supreme Council. I attended the F. U. M. Commission meetings as president, the meetings lasting from eight o'clock on to one or two o'clock in the morning.

I wrote a guide to the subordinate lodges which contained the directing principles for the subodinate lodges and the Grand Lodge.

I attended on September 1, 1925, as trial counsel a case in Oyster Bay in which there was involved a dispute caused by a division in a subordinate lodge at Oyster Bay. The Nuovo Vessillo of the 12th day of September, 1925, has an account of the case.

Memorandums, Briefs and Articles Written by Robert Ferrari.

Nuovo Vessillo, December, 1925, to January, 1926; 6 instalments of article. "Sons of Italy. A history." 10,000 words.

December, 1925—Article on The Function and Future of the Italians in the United States.

December, 1925—Articles on the F. U. M.

Law Writing—1. Memorandum, 10 pages. 2. Brief, 47 pages.

Speeches reported in Nuovo Vessillo, October 17, 1925, Corriere d'America, October 6, 1925.

CHRONOLOGIES

Chronology of Events

1. I enter the Order May 14th, 1925.
2. Elected by my Lodge, Fratelli Uniti, alternate delegate to the Grand Lodge Convention, June 11th, 1925.
3. I attend the Schenectady Convention August 5th to 8th, 1925.
4. August 6th, secession from the Grand Lodge, Order Sons of Italy in America, of the Sons of Italy, Grand Lodge Group, which held its convention in the City of New York.
5. I am elected president of the F. U. M. of the Schenectady Group.
6. I am appointed counsel to the Grand Lodge of the Schenectady Group.
7. Monthly meetings to the 14th of December, 1925, of the F. U. M.
8. Crisis meeting—or meeting which broke the camel's back, January 12, 1926.
9. January 15, 1926, combined meeting of the Grand Council and F. U. M. Commission.
10. January 22, 1926, meeting of the F. U. M. Commission including the up-state men.
11. January 29, meeting of the F. U. M. Commission, at which the loan of $2,500 for the payment of attorneys' fees, was voted by the F. U. M. Commission upon the recommendation of the Grand Council to the F. U. M.

CHRONOLOGY OF THE CONTROVERSY BETWEEN THE GRAND COUNCIL AND THE MORTUARY COMMISSION
and
ROBERT FERRARI,

After his resignation: February 3, 1926, to April 19, 1926.

Feb. 3, 1926—Resignation of Robert Ferrari from the Presidency of the F. U. M.; withdrawal from the position of counsel to the Grand Lodge; and resignation from the Subordinate Lodge, "Fratelli Uniti."

Mar. 28, 1926—Meeting of the Grand Council and the F. U. M. Commission for the purpose of deciding upon a communication to the Press, concerning the resignation of Robert Ferrari.

Mar. 28, 1926—Meeting of the Grand Council and the F. U. M. and communication to the press, authorized by the Grand Council and the M. F.

April 6, 1926—My reply; interview in the Nuovo Mondo to Ernest Valentini.

April 7, 1926—Statement of Robert Ferrari in the Nuovo Mondo and in La Follia.

April 16, 1926—Letter of the Grand Council to the Press, replying to my statement and interview of April 6th and 7th.

April 19, 1926—Circular 21 containing the communication to the Press of April 16th and the addition of introductory matter.

April 23, 1926—2nd Interview to Ernest Valentini published in the Nuovo Mondo.

April 26, 1926—Communication of the F. U. M. to the Press published in Corriere d'America.

May 4, 6 and 7—Reply to communication of F. U. M. of April 26th, in the Nuovo Mondo.

THE CHRONOLOGY OF LETTERS OF ROBERT FERRARI TO THE MORTUARY COMMISSION.

Dates of Letters by Me to the Secretary and Other Members of the Commission and to the Grand Venerable and Summary of Subject of These Letters.

Aug. 31, 1925—Letter to the Assistant Secretary, asking for every day notes of the state of the fund and of the events at the office.

Oct. 6, 1925—Hypersensibility of the Secretary of the Commission: Secretary complains of my praise of the Acting Secretary of the Grand Council. I reply.

Oct. 8, 1925—Letter of thanks to the Editor of the Corriere for having published my communication concerning the rights of combatants and of neutrals—a letter which attempted to keep a balance between the parties in spite of my engagement in the struggle and which endeavored to set forth the rights of the rank and file of the Order, who were the chief sufferers because of the bickerings of the leaders.

Nov. 4, 1925—Letter to the Assistant Secretary, desiring him to show me all matter intended for publication and complaining of a communication to the Press from the Commission, appearing on the 4th of November.

Nov. 6, 1925—Letter to the Secretary concerning two death benefit cases before the Commission, giving my reasons for not acting upon the papers submitted.

Dec. 18, 1925—Letter to the Secretary complaining of the inaccuracy of the minutes and of the payment by the Commission for unauthorized services.

Dec. 18, 1925—Letter to the Assistant Secretary asking him

to come to my office and show me all bills, letters and circulars written by members of the commission or employees.

Jan. 11, 1926—Letter to the Secretary complaining of the inaccuracy of the minutes and setting forth my objection to the granting of a loan of $2,500. My complaint concerning the inaccuracy of the minutes in respect to the happenings before the Commission in regard to the Italian Hospital.

Jan. 19, 1926—Letter to the Acting Secretary of the Grand Council concerning the meeting of Jan. 22nd.

Jan. 28, 1926—Letter to the Grand Venerable, expressing desire to resign.

Feb. 3, 1926—Letter to the Venerable of the Subordinate Lodge, "Fratelli Uniti," resigning from the Lodge.

Feb. 3, 1926—Letter of resignation to the Grand Venerable from the position of President of Mortuary Fund and Counsel to the Grand Lodge.

CHRONOLOGY OF "HONORARY PRESIDENCY" OF STEPHEN MIELE

Jan. 5, 1926—Circular 15 of the Grand Council. His name appears as Honorary President.

Feb. 10, 1925—Circular No. 17. His name is taken off.

CHAPTER I.

THE FLAME

EXPOSITION AND ARGUMENT
OF THE ACTION

Patriotism is the last refuge of a scoundrel.—Samuel Johnson.
We were not the first that ever burst
Into that silent sea.—Coleridge.
    Ye gentlemen of England
    That live at home at ease
    Ah! Little do you think upon
    The dangers of the seas.—Martyn Parker.
Kitty: Shikspur? Shikspur? Who wrote it?
    No, I never read Shikspur.
Lady Bab: Then you have an immense pleasure to come.—
    J. Townley.
No man knows so well where the shoe pinches as he who wears it.—Lincoln.
To found a great empire for the sole purpose of raising up a

people of customers is a project fit only for a nation of shopkeepers.—Adapted from Adam Smith.

Something is rotten in the state of Denmark.—Shakespeare.

A darned long row to hoe.—Lowell.

Row, brothers, row, the stream runs fast
The rapids are near and the daylight's past.—T. Moore.

With ruin upon ruin, rout on rout
Confusion worse confounded.—Milton.

We ain't no thin red heroes, nor we ain't no blackguards, too,
But single men in barricks, most remarkable like you;
An' if sometimes our conduck isn't all your fancy paints;
Why, single men in barricks don't grow into plaster saints.—
Kipling.

She wore a wreath of roses,
The night that first we met.—T. H. Bayly.

Why don't the men propose, mamma,
Why don't the men propose.—T. H. Bayly.

Full of sound and fury
Signifying nothing.—Macbeth.

I'd rather be a dog and bay the moon
Than such a Roman.—Julius Caesar.

What do you know of England
Who only England know.—........................

THE FLAME

Exposition and Argument

Circular No. 21 of the Grand Lodge of the State of New York, Order Sons of Italy in America, 27 Cleveland Place, is directed to all the venerable and brothers of the lodges and is a communication of the Grand Council. In this circular there is published a letter which appeared in the press and which was an answer to my statement and to an interview given to Ernest Valentini and an introduction to this letter. This gives me an opportunity not only of answering the charges brought there against me but also the opportunity of presenting my connection with the Order Sons of Italy in America.

This seems to have become necessary. It is inadvisable for me to keep on answering the communications which these people send to the press and which they publish in circular form. They have nothing else to do except that. I am a professional man and have to devote myself to professional work. I have given a great deal of time to the Order Sons of Italy as president of the F. U. M. and as counsel to the Grand Lodge, and after my resignation I thought I should be completely disassociated from them and be free to devote myself to my daily occupations.

After my resignation on the 3rd of February, 1926, I remained silent for two months in spite of the fact that lots of opportunity offered itself to speak and in spite of the fact also that there was great provocation as well as inducement to speak. Notwithstanding, I took no part in the discussion of the affairs of the Order Sons of Italy and did not discuss the matter even with my most intimate friends. These thought I had done the right thing and respected my dislike to talk upon a matter which had disgusted and nauseated me. Those who knew the reasons for my resignation could not but think that those reasons were sound and completely justificatory of my action.

The fact that I resigned on the 3rd of February, 1926, is not to be taken as absolute proof that it was only on the third day of February that I made up my mind to resign or that I had only then any desire to withdraw from the F. U. M., as counsel to the Grand Lodge and from the Order Sons of Italy in America. It was very soon after I entered upon my duties as president of the F. U. M. that I became convinced that I was in the wrong place. But being in it was a great question as to how to get out. The wise-acres who make everything in life simple and who have a remedy for every grievance and a way of escape for every difficulty—for other people—when they cannot give themselves proper advice or act in proper fashion, might say: "If you had made up your mind to leave why didn't you leave?"

The problem is not so simple. After being in it was necessary to look around to adjust myself if possible, and if I could not adjust myself, to leave with dignity and honor. Furthermore, it was necessary for me to have not only a valid excuse for myself for leaving the Order, but an excuse which would be valid for the public at large. The Order Sons of Italy is a public institution. It is the most powerful organization of Italians in the United States. It is known all over the country; its members run up to, it is said, three hundred thousand. There are three millions of Italians in the United States and directly or indirectly these three millions of Italians are connected with the Order Sons of Italy in America through the membership of that Order. It was proper then for me to remain in the Order just so long as I considered it necessary to obtain strong and lambent reasons which would be convincing and persuasive to the Italian world at large that I was justified in leaving the position of president of the F. U. M. and in retiring completely as counsel and as member of the Order Sons of Italy in America.

Fortunately for me and I hope fortunately also for those who are interested in the Order I remained long enough, six months, to have acquired sufficient information and knowledge of the affairs and of the men of the Order to make it possible for me to discuss these men and things with first hand information and intelligence.

The world would not have understood my leaving and would have considered it probably as the abandonment of my duty to the Order and to the Italians in America, if I had left before I had had proof—definite, certain, powerful—that the affairs of the

Order are not administered in the proper and regular way, and that the men who now dominate the Order and put their impress upon that Order are men unworthy of the respect of the Italians in the United States.

Circular No. 21 in its introductory part makes a great many statements which are known by the individuals who sent it out to be untrue. I am going to present a dilemma to the members of the Grand Council who got the circular out. They either knew of the falsity of the statements made in the circular or they did not know and were imposed upon by someone who sent it out without their knowledge. I cannot believe that Freschi; I cannot believe that Angrisani; or the up-state members of the Grand Council knew of the contents of the circular before it was sent out. If they did not, they were imposed upon just as the gang tried to impose upon me. They tried to make a decorative figure of me but they found out within two hours after the first meeting that they had someone to deal with. And yet the doubt arises in my mind as to whether they could have been ignorant of the fact that this circular was gotten up and sent out. It has been out over a week at the time of this writing and yet not a single statement has come out written by any one of these men repudiating Circular No. 21. Can it be that this Order because of the dominating influences upon it mars all it touches? Can it be that the contaminating influence of the Order because of the individuals who run it is potent and inevitable?

The circular gives me an opportunity of relating my connection with the Order Sons of Italy at the same time that I answer the charges brought against me. I came to know the men of the Order very well and know exactly whom I am dealing with at the present time. I know that they will stop at nothing to gain their ends. From the circulars that have been sent to the members of the lodges, from the communications that have gone to the press, from the conversations I have heard, I am more than ever convinced they are persuaded that they must either hang together or hang separately. And feeling this way and willing to use any weapon no matter how low and base, and willing to succeed no matter with what means, the end, namely, success, justifies any means they may use. I am dealing therefore, with a desperate lot. I must borrow from Goldsmith and stoop—a little—to conquer. Even this is a concession and a debasement from the elevated position I should like to occupy even in a combat with a ferocious and deadly enemy.

These men are conscious of the fact that there is a fool, as Barnum said, born every minute. From their convesations and from their acts I know also this, that they believed that Barnum was wrong—wrong in the fact that he thought only one fool was born a minute. They think a hundred are born every second. Therefore, they can say the most outrageous and the most extravagant things and feel that there is somebody in the world who will listen to them and will be taken in by them.

In this circular they sing the same song—the song that they have sung whenever anyone has tried to do something for the Order and who has been deceived, imposed upon, maltreated and crushed by the enemies of the Order within the Order and the enemies of the Italians in this country. They raise the cry of tyranny—tyranny not on their part, but tyranny upon mine. I who have allowed the utmost freedom of expression and of action, I who have given more freedom to others while I occupied the position of president of the F. U. M. than I gave to myself. Nobless oblige; the fact that I was in a position of power caused me to be mild, lenient and sympathetic of others who happened to be without. It is usually the individuals who are tyrannous who accuse others of being tyrannical.

They are wild because the opposition has published my statement and interviews. But certainly, they ought not to blame me for that. Their mentality is such however, that they do. They are like those individuals who offend others and then consider it an offense if the others retaliate. Or even without retaliation consider that they have been offended by the other if, and when, they offend that other. It happens in this case that I resigned without giving the reasons for my resignation. In doing that I wanted to prevent, because of a sense of delicacy, the repetition of the charges I had brought against the officials of the Order in private conversation and to committees. I am now charged with terrible and blasting crimes because I didn't give my reasons in my letters of resignation. But they well know it was due to the desire on my part not to have anybody take advantage of the fact of my resigning. The time had not come to speak. The time might have come and when it did I certainly should have spoken—just as the time did come and I did speak. I remained silent for two months and did not, as I say, speak even to my most intimate friends concerning the causes that had led to my resignation. I had ideas for the Order. I had ideals. I was disillusioned because of what I saw, I found it impossible to do things that should have been done for the Order and for the Italians in the United States. Just so long as the individuals at the head of the Order continue to dominate the Order or to be dominated by the real powers behind the throne, just so long will the Order be in a morass and the Italians wallow in the mud.

But when in the latter part of March there appeared a communication in the press saying that I had left the F. U. M. Commission not for general reasons concerning the administration of the Commission and the Order but for personal reasons and implied that I had not only signed a check for $2,500 to be given by the F. U. M. as a loan to the Grand Council for attorneys' fees but actually voted in favor of the granting of that loan, it was impossible for me any longer to keep silence. Did they wish to have a free field in which to hack and saw without feeling the retaliation of the injured party? Did they feel that I should have kept quiet and let them retail their nefarious untruths concerning my acts as president of the F. U. M. and as a man?

It was only then that I spoke—and I have been speaking ever since. I give them full warning that I shall continue to speak until the individual Miele who dominates the Order and dominates the individuals in the Order has been knocked off his pedestal and the Order put in the hands of individuals properly fitted for the guidance of such organizations as the Order Sons of Italy in America ought to be.

This matter rises beyond and above individuals into the realm of masses—into the realm of races and peoples. Individuals have to be dethroned not because of themselves as individuals but because we must prevent their action in environments and circumstances which produce either good or evil to a large community like the community of Italians in the United States.

Oh, the barefacedness of these people! They talk of the "triumph of truth and of justice" and the "respect for law" and that "might must triumph over right." It is a most screaming farce to hear these people talk in this way. They would not know justice or truth if they saw it. And yet they speak about representing justice and truth. They use and exercise force and do not know anything at all about right and yet they talk about the conquest of might by right. They violate the law, statute and moral—and yet they say they are upholders of law and of morality. They even have the supreme effrontery to go before the world and say they have a right to use a trust fund lent to the F. U. M. Commission with which to pay death benefits, for the purpose of paying attorneys' fees with. They violate morality and the decencies of life and they come out boldly before the world and say that they have done no wrong. It is difficult to know how to combat such men. They cannot be vanquished by argument because no argument can possibly reach them. They cannot be vanquished by shame, because they have none. The only thing we can do is to present the facts to an impartial world and allow that impartial world not only to judge for itself of their acts, but to act upon that judgment.

They say they have "elevated" me to the position, me who was unknown to the Order, to the high position of president of the F. U. M. Elevated me to the position of a hornet's nest where a Dantean bufera infernale, an infernal hurricane was raging. But they do not tell you that this elevation was not for my benefit but for theirs. They do not tell you that they begged me to take the position. They do not say how often at the Schenectady Convention they offered me the position of Grand Orator and that I refused. They do not tell the world that I refused the position of President of the F. U. M. when it was offered to me; and that it was difficult for them, a group of three or four, to cause me to consent. They do not say that they asked me to take it because they wanted the prestige of my name and not because they wanted to confer a benefit upon me. Elevate me to the high position of President and make me a most important personage in the affairs of the world! This is too much. I knew the height of their hypocrisy and the height of their feigning but it is almost inconceivable that evil human nature can further go.

I went up to Schenectady without seeking anything. Indeed, up to the very last moment before the boat left for Schenectady on which the delegates were going, I had not decided to go. They do not tell you that for weeks before this Schenectady Convention they kept on asking me to go to the meetings at the Pennsylvania Hotel, of the Group that remained solid with the Supreme Lodge.

They do not tell you that I never attended one of their meetings because I was bent upon remaining neutral in the fight between them and the Sons of Italy Grand Lodge. They do not tell you that they came to my office to consult me and try thus to drag me in, but failed. They want the world to ignore the fact that I was asked to prosecute as special trial counsel the officers of the Grand Council of the Sons of Italy Grand Lodge and that I declined. They keep silent concerning the fact that over and over again I was asked whether I was going to Schenectady and that I declined to give the answer they wished. Up to the very morning of the date previous to the Convention I had not decided to go. Certain events which happened—in which no individual in this Schenectady group had a part—certain documents and telegrams published the very last days before the Convention, and whatever documents and reports of proceedings which I could lay hands upon, having to depend upon my unaided efforts, which I read the night of August 4, 1925, made me decide to take the boat for Albany.

I was so careful to remain neutral, so bent on keeping out of the fight and so scrupulous about knowing all sides that I invited to my office a few days before the Convention and listened for over two hours to Sardi, Venerable of my subordinate lodge and Siani, Secretary—to hear the side of the Sons of Italy Grand Lodge and, I hoped, an impartial narration. (See letter App. 4).

On the boat I do not think I knew any more than three or four men. Indeed, I do not think I had any more than a dozen friends in the whole Order. Conversation with one man on the boat whom I knew brought me in touch with several other delegates and it was these delegates that did a great deal of propaganda work for me. They immediately asked me to take part on committees and I worked there for four consecutive days, day and night. I was part of the legal committee. I was part of the publicity committee and one or two other committees—work enough for any one man. It was after the delegates recognized what I was doing that people thought I should have some position in the Order. I thought it was better for me not to take any position. But the stream ran against that. I particularly objected to the position of president of the F. U. M. knowing how delicate that position would be and knowing what pressure would be brought to bear upon it and the consequences which would be produced becase of an immediate clash that would certainly arise. When I found that there was no way of escape; when I found that the unanimous opinion of the delegates was that I be president of the F. U. M.; when I discovered the fact that they wanted new men—and Ernest Valentini, editor of Zarathustra, in the first article he wrote immediately after the Convention made a profound observation when he said that the men in Schenectady needed new blood and so they looked for rescue to it—I accepted. They needed me and they gave me the privilege of being elevated to the position! Knowing them as I do now, they would not have given me or anybody like me, an opportunity of rising if they had felt that they were doing a service to me and not a necessary and pressing service to themselves. They tried to use me, me and my hard won reputation and my prestige for their purposes; but they found they could not subdue me to their will, mould me to their heart's desire. They found on the contrary that I was not only resistant material but that I would more easily mould them to my desire than they could mould me to theirs. The clash had to come. The crash came. It was only a question of time. It might have been two months. It might have been three or six or twelve. All was in the laps of the gods and all depended upon how long the opposition would retain control of its head. If they forced the issue immediately they would have an immediate adverse reaction, an immediate combat and an immediate revolution. It took four months before matters came to a head on the most important question that came before the Commission, the granting of a loan of $2,500 and the granting of another loan of $1,700 for the payment of expenses of Grand Delegates to Washington. It took two more finally to resolve the question of my staying in the Order or going out. I had been in the Order before the Convention only for three months and I admit therefore, I was unknown in the Order. But this destroys completely the argument that I joined the Order Sons of Italy because I "desired publicity for myself as I confessed on divers occasions." If I was unknown what could I have hoped for? I had a long road to hoe. I had a high and rough hill to climb—unless they think that I am a super-man and in spite of all my handicaps I could do in a few months what it would have taken other people twenty years to do. They may not be mistaken!

But to think of the utter idiocy of a Grand Council which puts into permanent printed form the statement that I confessed on various occasions that I had entered the Order to get publicity for myself because I needed it! To whom did I confess this? Certainly to no member of the Grand Council. If I confessed it to anybody else let the Grand Council name the man.

Desired publicity of which I was in need and therefore entered the Order Sons of Italy with the fixed thought of conquering the most important position in the Order and elevating myself upon the backs of the Order to some distinguished position in the community! So far as publicity is concerned I have gotten all the publicity in my life which I desire. Only a few months before the Convention in August I had more publicity than any member of the Grand Council will ever have or the whole Grand Council combined. I had tried a criminal case and my name had been in one of the morning papers, "The World," every single day for a whole month and in all the papers every day for over two weeks. Did I need publicity? Ten millions of people at least, had seen my name and heard of my doings and yet I wanted some position in the Order Sons of Italy three months before the Convention to get publicity for myself and therefore I joined the Order.

But even if it were true, is it not legitimate to have that laudable ambition of becoming something in such an Order as the Sons of Italy in America—if that Order be on so elevated a plane as the members of the Grand Council consider it to be because of their direction of it? Who would blame me as who would blame any member of the Grand Council for desiring to be a member of the Grand Council?

I am a realist in politics, and would not for a moment hesitate to say that I desired to obtain control of conditions in order to make concrete my ideas. I do not hesitate now to say that I did have illusions when I entered the Order; that those illusions were due to the fact that I did not know the men who had control of it. I did think that something could be done with the Order to make it an exponent and a representative of the Italians and a power among them and among the communities in which they are. I do not even conceal the fact that I had a vague intangible and far off idea that I might be one of the humble instruments for the making of the Order a power in America for the benefit and salvation of the Italians. Is this reprehensible? Yet I could not, unless I be a clairvoyant, see such a rapid rise to the position of president of the F. U. M. or any position equivalent to that in power in so short a time. I dare say that if the Order had remained united I should not have risen so rapidly. There were conditions and circumstances which would have prevented that. The Order would not have needed me so badly. It was the fact of civil war that caused a breakdown of the machinery of government in the Order and made possible a meteoric change in conditions; a change of which I took advantage. I took occasion by the forelock and bent it to my will. I was no passive instrument in the hands of these old foxes and diplomats. They had better know that if they have not already found it out as old foxes and old diplomats.

They charge me with being a metaphysician and restive under the practicalities of life. But had I not been that metaphysician

I could not have used them as they tried to use me. The ogres tried to frighten me and eat me up; and it was the ogres themselves who were eaten. By this time they know that metaphysicians when they come in conflict with practical men are dangerous personages.

They say that I wished to destroy every authority in the Order. If I had done that; if I had wished that, I should not have wished something improper. When the power that directs is infected there is no reason for respecting it, but there is all the reason in the world for overthowing it.

They charge me with tyranny and they say that the only tyranny involved is the tyranny that I used upon the employees of the office whom I made my slaves and my messengers. I gave a great deal to the Order. I gave of time and money; time and money when I could ill afford it. Even supposing I had used some of those employees of the F. U. M., would it not be ungrateful for the Grand Council and the Order to throw it up to me now? But the fact is that whenever I used them for my personal work—and this personal work during the six months I was connected with the Order did not take any more than four or five hours to accomplish—I paid the individuals who ran the errands for me.

The tyranny that they complain of, the tyranny that sticks in their throat is the tyranny of my objection to do their will. If this is tyranny let them make the most of it. I did object and objected strenuously to a great many things they wanted me to do. I did object and objected strenuously to the granting of the two loans because I considered those loans improper, irregular, illegal and immoral. If I had been subdued to what I worked in; if I had been bent to their pleasure, they would not now be accusing me of tyranny. It wasn't that I was an autocrat; it wasn't that I tried to impose my will upon them that causes them to say that I was tyrannical. It was only because they attempted to impose their will upon me and failed.

To show how perfectly ridiculous their position is let me quote a letter which I wrote to Freschi the Grand Venerable immediately preceding the Washington Convention and after the critical meeting of January 12, 1926, at which Miele had come for the second time to the F. U. M. Commission to propose a loan of $2,500 and in addition, at that meeting proposed a loan of $1,700 for the payment of the expenses of the Grand Delegates to Washington. I had for about two months previous to January 12th prevented, and did for two weeks after that date prevent the granting of the loans and there was a tremendous revolution within our group caused by the terror that they would not be able to gather the $25,000 which the attorneys had asked as a retainer. If the State of New York could not pay its quota of $2,500 then the other states would not pay. If the State of New York went to Washington without a check for $2,500 there would be no possibility, they argued, that the other states would be interested in an action pending in the State of New York begun by the Order Sons of Italy in America.

They, therefore, were accusing me of autocracy because I did not desire to grant the loan and because I was standing out against the unanimous current moving in the opposite direction.

I sent the Grand Venerable the following letter which will show my state of mind and my desire to resign, but also the fact that I was against the granting of the loans and that autocracy, moral coercion and physical compulsion had been used upon me by members of the Order—the arch offender being Miele.

Hon. John Freschi,   January 28, 1926.

50 Pine Street, New York City.

Dear John:

I have been reliably informed that it is the general opinion of people among our group of the Order Sons of Italy that in declining to grant a loan from the Mortuary Fund in order to pay attorneys with and to grant another loan of $1,700 for the payment of the expenses of the Supreme delegates to Washington, I have been acting in an autocratic manner and as an enemy of the Order.

This is simply outrageous. If anybody should complain of autocracy it is I. I have given other people full liberty to express their ideas and I have taken the right to do myself what I have accorded others the right to do. Others, however, have attempted to gain their ends by moral coercion and physical compulsion. If we have not seen eye to eye, it is unfortunate, but certainly I should not be blamed in this fashion.

I do not desire to obstruct your proceedings in any manner. I am therefor willing, indeed eager at the present moment, and before the convention meets, to hand in my resignation to take effect immediately.

I shall give my reasons to an impartial world and let that world judge between my oponents and me.

RF/RJ   Cordially yours,

They tell you that I had no program, social or cultural. They tell you that I never referred to that program and that I kept it within my own head because I was afraid somebody would steal the copyright from me. This charge is put in large letters and is repeated two or three times. These men are incorrigible. They are either wicked, conscious tellers of untruths or they are egregious ignoramuses. Members of the Grand Council have been present when I have developed my social and cultural program and when I have elaborated my ideas concerning the work of the Order and the work of the Italians of the United States. Members of the Grand Council have read my articles in which I have developed and amplified the same things. Or at least, I hope they have done me the honor and taken the trouble to read the articles I have written. If they have not read them let me indicate to them a few places where they may be enlightened.

The Corriere d'America of October 16, 1925, contains a very brief yet pregnant account of a lecture I delivered at the inauguration of the Lodge Nicola Misasi on October 14, 1925, at the Sons of Italy Hall, on East 15th street.

"There followed Counsellor Ferrari who improvised a learned lecture on the problems of the Order and of the community." The Nuovo Vessillo of October 17th, 1925, contained a more elaborate account of the same speech.

At this inauguration, Paul Vitali, one of the old war horses of the Order, said in his speech that what he had heard fall from my mouth during the last hour had given him more instruction and inspiration than all he had heard and all he had seen in the Order for four years previous.

I wrote an article called "Sons of Italy. A history" in which I gave a social and cultural program for the Order and tried to indicate the problems the Order would have to solve in the American community and how best to solve them. This article ran in six installments in the Nuovo Vessillo beginning December, 1925, and ending January, 1926. I also harped on the unity of the Italians and regretted the split of the Order in this state.

I direct the attention of the Grand Council particularly to the issue of January 9, 1926, page 1, second column.

"What is the present position of the Italian group in this country in relation to other groups? What ought its position to be with respect to other groups? What contribution should be made to American life by the Italian group? How should that contribution be made? Should the Italian group and the other groups be allowed absolute and unfettered freedom to develop, and make their contribution, or should they be cribbed, cabined and confined by restrictions placed upon them by the American government, or by any group, racial or economic in this country.

"The hope of the America of the future lies in the fostering and the cherishing of the American born of foreign descent because he is the reflection of the environment in which he lives and in which he has been brought up; and this environment is the American Scene.

"They hold that we have enough problems and difficulties of our own to solve in this country. Our thoughts should be directed to solving them as being the immediate objects of our environment, and as being pressing elements for our good or evil—for our happiness or misery."

I direct their attention also to the article on "The Functions and The Future of The Italians in America" in the Nuovo Vessillo of December, 1925.

I direct the attention of the Grand Council also to the following letter which I wrote to Mr. Garbellano in which I speak of the pressing need for unity among the Italians in America and of the function of the Italians in this country—a function that the Order could under proper management perform.

Mr. F. Garbellano,   November 7, 1925.

Sons of Italy Hall, 109 East 15th St., New York City.

Dear Brother Garbellano:

Many happy years of life to the Sons of Italy Hall. At last the Italians in the City of New York have a place they can call their home. May the tenderest sentiments cling around that home. In this country of ours far away from the land of our fathers, or the land of our birth, we must try to be worthy of the traditions and the history that have made the Ialian what he is. But we must wear our flowers of joy as well as our rue with a difference. Above all things, we should strive after distinction, dignity and elevation. Let the Sons of Italy Hall be a place where souls bruised with adversity or favored by fortune may seek and find comfort and rest of spirit. Let the Sons of Italy Hall be the means of uniting in one harmonious family, the Italians of this city, as a prelude to the unification of the Italians in the State of New York and in the United States. Let the sons and daughters of that land which has the fatal gift of beauty transmute that fatal gift in the environment of the new world into a magic contribution to the mind and heart of America.

Beauty and truth and sympathy is a combination and a form indeed which America will highly prize. He teaches best who feels the hearts of all men in his breast and knows their strength and weakness in his own.

The understanding and the sympathetic heart of the Italian will go far toward comprehending the minds and the hearts of the people of other races in this country and will more easily and more vigorously bring about the harmony and unification of the various races living together in America.

RF/W   Cordially and Fraternally yours,

CHAPTER II.

RISE OF THE ACTION
and
CLIMAX—

Lives like a drunken sailor on a mast,
Ready with every nod, to tumble down
Into the fatal bowels of the deep.—Shakespeare.
A sadder and a wiser man
He rose the morrow morn.—Coleridge.
Of all sad words of tongue or pen.
The saddest are these: "It might have been."—Whittier.
The Exploiters of the Order at work—
Hierarchy of the Order.
That's a valiant flea that dare eat his breakfast on the lip of
a lion.—Shakespeare.
So naturalists observe, a flea
Has smaller fleas that on him prey;
And these have smaller still to bite 'em;
And so proceed ad infinitum.—Swift.
And the grossness of his nature will have
Weight to drag thee down.—Tennyson.

Miele

Oh! for a forty-parson power to chaunt
Thy praise, hypocrisy.—Byron.
Shylock.   Is that the law?—Shakespeare.
Thou petty katydid!—Adapted from Holmes.
A kick, that scarce could move a horse,
May kill a sound divine.—Cowper.
The fattest hog in Epicurus' sty.—William Mason.
It must not be; there is no power in Venice,
Can alter a decree established;
'Twill be recorded for a precedent
And many an error by the same example
Will rush into the State; it cannot be.—Shakespeare.
The time when screech-owls cry, and ban-dogs howl,
And spirits walk, and ghosts break up their graves.—Shake-
speare
Pygmies are pygmies still, though perched on Alps,
And pyramids are pyramids in vales.—Young.

CHAPTER II.

RISE OF THE ACTION

and

CLIMAX—

Crisis—Meeting, January 12, 1926.

All these things I have related, may not, in the minds of some people, be sufficient to cause me to turn upon the man who is the arch culprit. There must be some peculiar personal motive forcing me on to attack Miele and to make him out to be a devil incarnate. If there ever was such a devil incarnate in human form, it is he. He is the evil spirit of the Order and has been during the whole time of its existence. I have had during fifteen years only a bowing acquaintance with him. I do not think I had spoken any more than fifty words altogether during the whole time I had known of his existence, yet I knew him as well as anybody could know another without contact. For the first few months, the Miele clan tried blandishments and verbal caresses. When they found that these could not serve their purpose, they used moral coercion and physical force. Pasquale Miele, one night on the corner of 116th Street, after he had taken me up in his automobile there from a meeting of the Mortuary Commission at 27 Cleveland Place, told me that very soon there would be a big banquet given to me and a one thousand dollar diamond ring presented me. Stephen Miele himself, in the presence of Panetta, while walking up Broadway, coming out of the American firm's office, the latter part of August, 1925, after I had devoted many hours every day as counsel to the case, said I would be able to make a great deal of money out of the business that would come to me through my connection with the Order Sons of Italy. He is an expert in exploiting the Order; and he thought everyone else had the same tenacious and voracious claws as he. I laughed a silent and ironical laugh in both cases, and after Miele in the second instance, left us I expressed to Panetta, the stupidity of a man who would speak in that fashion, first, because it was impossible for a man like me to make any money out of the Sons of Italy, and second because he could think that such a statement would influence me.

I came into close association with the members of the Mortuary Fund and the Grand Council and he was omnipresent. I had to come into close association with him, not because I desired it, but because I had to. My great regret is that in trying to do good and entering the Order to make my contribution to the advancement of the Order and the Italians in this country, I was forced to come into close association with him. Yet I always treated him with consideration and with the outward, though distant amenities of life. Indeed, he had spread the news that I hated him. This was back in August, a couple of weeks after the Convention. Why these underground whisperings? Because we had begun to differ in our concepts and in our methods of action and he was forging his alibi and his defense.

The man had begun to take as personal offense, even the giving of my opinion on principle and policy before the Committee of Lawyers and the Committee of Laymen. You had to follow his way out or you became a deadly enemy of his. It was because he had spread this underground news that I was outwardly more disposed to give him the appearance of consideration before other people. And therefore, whenever I had to oppose an opinion of his, I did it in as impartial and unimpassioned a manner as possible.

On the 12th of January occurred the meeting which I refer to as the crisis-meeting. He had appeared before the Committee on the 14th day of December, 1925, and had for the first time presented the proposal of the loan for $2,500 to the Grand Council. I opposed the proposal for various reasons, which I indicated in a letter written on the 11th of January to the Secretary of the Commission. The 14th day of December was the first time I heard anything about that loan, although it had been decided at a meeting of the Supreme Council at which the Grand Venerables of the various states had been invited, including Freschi. Miele of course tho not a Grand Venerable had made one of the number. Miele and Freschi had decided, after discussion at that meeting, to ask the Mortuary Fund for the loan. I was not consulted. By that time, differences of temperament and of background had had their effect and Miele was trying to run the whole show. Indeed, first because I was thoroughly sick of going to a great many useless meetings, and second, because I was a disturbing element in those meetings, they tried to do things without me and therefore, did not even invite me to some of the meetings, which they held, lawyers and laymen. So it was that it was only on the 14th day of December, that I was surprised to learn that they wanted the money out of the Mortuary Fund. They were not drawing upon their own treasury in taking funds for fees, but they were putting the Members of the Commission and me, particularly as President, in a very delicate, and serious position. Aside from the fact that such a demand upon the Commission would have been highly irregular at any time, even in time of peace, it certainly was extremely irregular now in time of civil war.

But it was, curiously enough, this very fact of civil war that egged them on to want to do things in the quickest and the shortest way, regardless of the legal or the moral aspects of the case.

When Miele presented himself before the Committee, therefore, to ask for a vote upon the loan, I allowed all the Commissioners to speak first and asked them one by one, their opinion as to whether the loan should be granted or not. I decided to give them full freedom to express their thought without prejudice caused by the indication of my own opinion. I found all the Commissioners perfectly willing to grant the loan. It was my business therefore, to expound to the Commission the reasons which had induced me to come to my conclusion.

Because of the attitude of Miele toward me and of his underground whisperings of my dislike for him, which began, be it remembered, way back in the month of August, I tried to keep as much peace and harmony within the Committee and the Order as I could, believing that while I was there I should make the most of the bad position I found myself in, I dealt with the objections I had to the loan in a calm, quiet, considerate way, which aroused the understanding and the sympathy of the other members of the commission, who decided upon my urgent request, to put the matter over to another meeting, in order to give me an opportunity of investigating further. If I thought that the loan ought to be granted, since there was tremendous pressure brought to bear upon the commission, as Miele and his gang were spreading the news that the American attorneys wanted an immediate fee of $25,000, or they would abandon the case and leave them all in the lurch, I was to call another meeting before the regular monthly meeting, if I considered it advisable. The next day after the meeting of December 14th and the following days, I made my investigation. I deliberated upon the subject, consulted, studied and finally, at the end of three days came firmly and definitely to the conclusion that the loan was highly improper and ought, under no circumstances to be granted, no matter what the pressure brought to bear and no matter how vital the loan was considered by Miele and his crowd for the purpose of carrying on the case. I felt personally, that Miele and the others who wanted me to grant the loan, were taking a dirty advantage of me in my position as President of the Mortuary Fund, in putting the screws on to squeeze out of me a loan, which on the very face of it, was a deviation of the trust fund for death benefits to a purpose foreign to the purpose for which the fund was established. The more you thought of it the worse it became, not only as a matter of principle but also as a personal matter to me and to the members of the Commission. It made no difference to members of the Grand Council perhaps, or to the Grand Venerable, what the action of the Commission was, inasmuch as the heavy primary responsibility was upon the members of the Commission and not upon those who had instigated the commission to commit the act. It made no difference, of course, to Stephen Miele, who is used to underground methods and who himself, said in the course of the meeting of January 12th, that nothing illegal or immoral would stop him from doing what he considered to be for the advantage of the position he had assumed. His long history in the Order had deadened him to the ordinary decencies of life. It meant nothing to him to ruin the Order and involve in that ruin people who had borne a spotless reputation. He had nothing to lose. He had already lost all. If I had acted swiftly as is my wont, if anybody has ever been justified in quick reaction, I would have been justified. Yet, I kept my counsel, took my medicine, being as I was, surrounded by conscious and unconscious enemies among the officials.

I explained my irrevocable decision to the officers of the Grand Council and to the members of the Mortuary Fund and even went so far as to speak of my discussion and consultation with an attorney in the case, whom I shall not name now. I therefore, did not hold any special meeting after the regular meeting of December 14th. I waited until the next meeting of January 12th when I thought the matter was not going to be presented any more. I reckoned without my host. Although I had written to the Secretary on January 11th, complaining of the putting of the question of the loan on the order of business and telling him that I was unalterably opposed to it and therefore, did not want it to remain in the order of business, the matter came up for discussion before the Commission and Miele was again there to remake the proposal. After I had allowed everybody to speak, including Miele, instead of cutting off discussion and crushing out all opposition by saying I was opposed and did not want to talk any more on the subject, I renewed my objections and tried to put them in a new light, adding such material as had come to me during the previous month. I had not talked long when Miele cut me off in a brusque way and said that there was no use talking about it and that I could do what I wanted.

A presiding officer, regardful of his duty as a presiding officer and as a man could not let that go unnoticed. I told him that it was unjust of him to try to cut off my speech when I had allowed him to go on to develop his ideas; that I had a right as a member of that commission upon whom the greatest responsibility lay, especially as the President happened to be a lawyer, to express my ideas in opposition to his own.

CHAPTER III.

ANSWER OF ROBERT FERRARI.

to the Communication published April 26, 1926, of the Mortuary

Fund ⸱ F. U. M. ⸱ of the Order Sons of Italy in America,

27 Cleveland Place

Whom the Gods would destroy they first make mad.
> **—From the Greek.**

Beware of entrance to a quarrel, but, being in
Bear it that the opposed may beware of thee.
> **—Hamlet.**

Touch nothing you do not adorn.   **—From the Latin.**

A communication from the F. U. M. of the Order Sons of Italy in America, 27 Cleveland Place, appeared in the "Corriere d'America" on the 26th of April, 1926 signed by the President of the F. U. M., F. Catinella, and by the Secretary.

This communication is an attempt to answer the charges which I made in a statement which I recently gave to the press and in an interview written by E. Valentini and published in the "Nuovo Mondo."

Mr. Catinella as the President of the F. U. M. cannot possibly know what had happened in the U. F. M. when I was President. In spite of this fact he signs the communication and makes such extravagant statements as the following: That the resolutions as indicated by the minutes of the F. U. M. are accurate and not false; and that it is not true that third parties—not members of the F. U. M.—have interferred with the business of the F. U. M. and tried to impose thier wishes upon the Commission.

It is impossible for Mr. Catinella or anybody else, except members of the Commission, to know whether the minutes are true or false or whether anybody not a member of the Commission has attempted to influence the Commission in regard to proposals before it. The present President of the F. U. M. knows, because I myself spoke to him before the Washington Convention and after the Washington Convention immediately after sending in my resignation on the third of February, 1926, of the constant interference on the part of Miele in the affairs of the Commission and of his persistent efforts

---

* F. U. M. means Mortuary Commission.

to cause the Commission to grant a loan of $2500, a loan which I considered illegal and immoral.

He also knows of my constant opposition for over two months to the granting of the loan for the payment of the attorneys in the case, and was present at the combined meeting of the 15th day of January, 1926, when the Grand Council and the F. U. M. met and discussed the question of the granting of the loan. At that meeting he knows very well that everybody in the Grand Council and in the F. U. M. was in favor of the granting of the loan and that he is the only man that supported me in my opposition to the granting of that loan. Afterwards within the next two or three days he changed his mind and he signed a statement with other members of the Grand Council recommending to the F. U. M. the granting of the loan. At this meeting of the F. U. M. Commission, called expressly by me for the purpose of discussing the question of the loan and putting the matter to a vote, telegrams from the upstate members of the Commission were read approving the granting of the loan. Every other member of the Commission was in favor of the granting of the loan. One member of the F. U. M. Commission was absent that night but he had already expressed his approval on numerous occasions before that meeting. I was the only one who stood out down to the very end and directed the Secretary as I had directed him on previous occasions to make a note of my objection to the granting of the loan and to my negative vote. Whatever precautions a human being could take I took; and the minutes of the F. U. M. Commission beginning from the 14th of December and running down to the very end of my incumbency were not signed by me, simply because of the fact that I objected to their inaccuracy. If these minutes are signed at the present time they certainly have not been signed by me. I am inform-ed that the new President has signed these minutes. It seems incon-ceivable to me—although anything is possible now that I know the people I have to deal with,—that the minutes of the Commission at which the granting of the loan was approved should read that my vote was in favor of the granting of the loan.

Fortunately everybody in the Order knew that I had been op-posed to that loan and everybody knew that I had voted against it at the time it was put to a vote. At Washington in caucus of the New York delegates, Freschi made the statement that the check for $2500 had been obtained from the F. U. M. Commission and that each person had voted according to his lights. Everybody understood this to be a reference to me because I had voted against the granting of the loan. When the Committee of the Grand eDlegates came down to see me at my office after I had resigned, I spoke to them at great length and in detail over a period of four hours and everybody there understood and knew from the members of the Commission and from the Grand Council and from me directly that I had not only objected to the granting of the loan but had voted against it at the final meet-ing.

M. Capparelli, the Editor of the "Nuovo Vessillo," knew two months before the voting of the coming of Miele to the Commission and the asking of a loan and my objection to it. I spoke to him for over two hours in my office, telling him the troubles of F. U. M. and explaining to him how it was impossible for me to continue any longer because of the things required of me and because of the coming of Miele into the Commission and disturbing our proceedings by the introduction of extravagant proposals and by pressure upon the members of the Commission. In addition to all these men, Panetta, who was acting secretary of the Grand Council, knew that from the beginning to the end I was opposed, and knows that when at the last moment I put the matter to a vote, I voted against. I could have avoided a vote immediately preceding the Washington Convention if I had wanted to; but I felt that I had no moral right to delay the vote any longer inasmuch as everybody was unanimous in favor of the granting of the loan. I had attempted for over two months to prevent what I considered to be an illegal and an immoral act. I did this not only to save the Commission and the Grand Council but to save the Order itself. However, there was no moral obbligation on my part to continue forever to be opposed and to prevent a vote upon the subject. As a matter of fact, my moral duty was, under the rules of parliamentary law and under the rules of good behavior, to put the matter to a vote and let the Order take the consequences of the act of the majority. Just as long as it could be proved that I had been opposed, that would be sufficient protection for the future. So it was that immediately preceding the convention when there was such an uproar on the part of the men connected with our group, who said that they would be destroyed if a check were not in Washington since the National Convention would say: "we do not propose to give any money to the lawyers because the State of New York, the most intimately involved, does not make any contribution itself," I put the matter to a vote. It was my duty as President therefore, after everybody had decided with the exception of myself, to grant the loan to the Grand Council for the payment of attorneys' fees, to put my signature to the check. If I had not done that I should have been guilty of an illegal act and moreover been guilty of an unmanly one. I find—and found very soon after I entered the Order— that I am dealing with a group that will stop at nothing to gain their ends. It was with this thought in mind, that I tried to protect myself even from the beginning. Loud and vociferous objection telling the secretary to record objections and negative votes in the minutes would not have been sufficient, as I soon found out, because the minutes did not exactly reflect the events that took place in the Commission. Loud and vociferous objection outside the Commission so that everybody might hear and know does not seem to have done any good either. For if one person knew that I had objected strenuously and had voted against, a hundred knew it. Yet in this last communication to the Press by the F. U. M., signed by the President and the Secretary of the Commission, there is the barefaced implication—mind you, again an implication, as in the first communication to the press—not an express statement, that I signed the check and voted in favor of the granting of the loan—the implication that I signed the check and did not vote in the negative. I should like to know what the minutes of that meeting show now, and whether the minutes show that I voted against the granting of the loan. I never saw those minutes. They were never submitted to me. The Wash-ington Convention took place two days after and immediately upon my return I sent in my letter of resignation to the Grand Venerable and these minutes were never submitted to me for signature. I have been told that they have been signed by the present President of the F. U. M. What they show I do not know. I should not be sur-prised to find anything there of the most extravagant and Baron Munchausen sort.

However that may be and whatever the minutes may show—minutes which I have never signed, contrary to the statement made in this last communication that all the minutes of the F. U. M. have been signed by me—this communication contains the statement that "Fer-rari, in order to have an excuse, should have sent in his resignation eight days earlier than he did or decline to sign the check in the same way in which he had declined to sign many other important and urgent matters of administration, that is, death benefits due, thus creating a strong discredit to the institution." There is nothing at all beyond these men. They will even go so far as to try to advise people what to do—men who are not capable of advising themselves. If they had been capable of advising themselves and one another, they certainly would not have granted a highly illegal loan of $2500 for the payment of attorneys' fees. Yet these men have the brazen faced-ness to try to advise me as to the time of my resignation.

They know as well as I do that I did not resign before the Wash-ington Convention not because I wasn't desirous of resigning then, even before the last meeting when the matter of the loan was put to a vote—and a letter which I have already given the contents of, will show this perfectly clearly—but because—ingratitude thy name is officials of the ORDERS SONS OF ITALY IN AMERICA!—I was trying to save them. (See Appendix 4 for letters). The unanimous current of opinion minus one, was that if New York did not present its quota of $2500 to the National Convention the other states would, like Achilles, sulk in their tents and would not contribute the quota which they had promised for the attorneys' retainer.

It made no difference to these individuals that for weeks I had presented to them various methods of raising the loan if they wanted to get the loan. I had told them that the money lent by the lodges to the F. U. M. was a trust fund which could be used only for the specific purposes for which the Fund was raised, as indicated in the resolution of the Grand Lodge where the F. U. M. was created. I told them that if they wanted the $2500 they could get it in one of various ways. They could get it by obtaining the authorization of the lodges that had made the loan for the purposes of the F. U. M. Commission. Or they could get a loan from the lodges on our side—a few dollars from each lodge would have made up the whole sum of $2500. Surely if this matter was a matter of life and death as Miele and the others represented it to be for New York State, they certainly could do either one of the two things which I, as President of the F. U. M., required. Again, I told them in Commission meet-ting after having presented all my objections during the space of one hour, that it was a responsibility and a liability which should not be placed either upon the President of the Commission or the members of the Commission and that if the worst came to the worst, I was willing to chip in and make my small contribution with a few others who could be gathered together to make up the whole sum of $2500. At this time, at the beginning of December, my financial condition made it possible for me to do it although a few weeks before it would have been out of the question for me to attempt it. I had devoted August, September, October and November to work for the Order Sons of Italy as President of the Commission and as counsel for the Grand Lodge and had worked day and night. The ordinary work in my office had been disorganized and had to be neglected because of the pressure of labor required. In addition to all this work, dozens of members of the Order called me up, many times during the day and a great many individuals from the lodges came to see me at my office, asking me all sorts of questions concerning their affairs. I might very easily have said, inasmuch as I had received no fee and inasmuch as few lawyers in the City of New York under modern conditions can work for four long months without a penny of remuneration, that if they wanted their $2500 they might get it elsewhere. Yet out of my meagre store, I said before the members of the Commission in the presence of Miele who was insisting upon his proposal for the granting of the loan by the Commission, that I was willing to make my small contribution with a few others in order to prevent the Commission from doing an illegal and an immoral act. Aside from the question of illegality, there was the moral obligation upon the members of the Commission and the members of the Grand Council before they took a cent from the F. U. M. or asked the F. U. M. to grant the payment of attorneys' fees, to ask, at least, the lodges or to inform them of the fact. Yet these men were willing not only to keep the masses of the Order in the dark, but were eager to put their iron hands upon the funds of the Order and lift these funds out of the treasury to pay attorneys' fees and expenses of Supreme Delegates with, for, it must be understood—and the communication here is again inexact—there was a strenuous and violent effort mode to take from the funds of the F. U. M. another sum of $1700 for the purpose of paying with that sum the expenses of the 35 delegates who were going to Washington.

In addition to all these possibilities for the raising of the $2500, it was not an extravagant thing to suppose that if the money could not be gotten in any other way, Miele should make a loan to the Grand Council. He was the chief beneficiary of the Order and is such at the present time, and there would not have been anything wild and impractical for him to have made the loan himself or to have endorsed a note which could have been discounted; and in this latter case the operation would have produced the money without his laying out a penny! (Ironical smile upon my lips. This stage direction for those without a sense of humor). I never presented this possibility to the Commission or to anybody else except to one individual whom I do not name at the present time but whom circumstances in the future may compel me to mention. Why, I said, is this

Miele so insistent upon forcing me and the Commission to grant this loan? Why does he come time after time? Why does he influence the members of the Commission, in the Commission and outside the Commission, to grant the loan? Why does he persevere in this obstinate course of his when I have indicated my objection over and over again? Why does he come before the Commission for the second time and present the same proposal when I have said one hundred times that I think the loan irregular, illegal and immoral and will not grant it? Why, in addition to all this, does he rub it in and when the proposal for the $2500 loan is in obeyance, ready to be taken up again and presented to the Commission by the same man at the first opportunity, why does he present another proposal to the Commission for a loan of $1700 for the payment of the expenses of the Supreme Delegates who were going to Washington? If I considered the first illegal, I certainly would consider the second illegal. And when I say the second proposal is illegal why does he continue to argue the matter and to make what was the critical scene immediately preceding the convention? If he was so much interested, certainly the importance of the matter should have prompted him to pay out of his own pocket. For all the noise he made and allth e persistence he manifested, the object would have been worth to him the sum of $2500.

They were so bent on getting the money from me that my constant objection in writing and by word of the mouth in the Commission and out of the Commission produced upon them no effect, except to make them redouble their efforts to get the money out of the Commission. It was only in the middle of January—on the day of the combined meeting of the Grand Council and the F. U. M.—that they got an opinion from an American lawyer who with others was handling their case, that the loan of $2500 could lawfully be made by the Commission but that the loan for the payment of the expenses of the Supreme Delegates could not lawfully be made. If these people who now write airy statements to the press had desired to proceed regularly, why, after I had objected in writing and by word of mouth, did they not seek the opinion of that lawyer before the middle of January? They were in daily and hourly contact with him. They did not dare. They knew it was wrong. They sought it only after my continued objection and after my prevention of a vote upon the subject. They did not want the opinion of lawyers because they thought that opinion would be adverse. It was only because they were finally forced that they got it; but before that Miele had appeared before the Commission to ask for the loans; and he appeared not, as the first communication to the Press and this last communication say, "only two times as the representative of the Grand Council." He appeared upon his own initiative without any recommendation or resolution of the Grand Council and not as the representative of the Grand Council.

He came at least three times altogether on the loans and he never got the authorization of the Grand Council until I had demanded he obtain an authorization of his appearance from the Grand Council.

I also demanded, fully to protect the helpless members of the

Commission, and to compel the responsibility of the Grand Council, a recommendation of the Grand Council, to the F. U. M. From the statements that have appeared in the press, these individuals of the F. U. M. don't deserve to be saved. But I did it as an act of humanity and do not now regret it. These members of the F. U. M. know definitely and positively that the statements made in the last communication published on the 26th day of April are untrue.

They heard the Commissioners. They heard the debates and they must know that the statements made are untrue. Again, Miele, the evil spirit of the Order, the dominant man of the Order, the man who puts the pressure upon the men of the Commission and upon the men of the Grand Council, the man who created the men of the Commission and the men of the Grand Council; again, I say, it is he who has been instrumental in causing the production of such an istrument as this last communication, which is the negation of all truth. To prove what I have said concerning the nefarious influence of this man upon the Order and upon the members of the Order and the debasing effects upon the individuals concerned of his machinations, I say now that even a man like Catinella has been caused to sign a document which he cannot know to be true or false. The communication says that Miele never said before the Commission, when he proposed the granting of the two loans at the meeting on the 12th of January 1926, three days before the combined meeting of the Grand Council and the F. U. M.; that "if illegal and immoral things had not been done in the Order, nothing would have been done." Of course the present President of the Commission cannot tell whether these words were spoken or not. Yet he signs the statement and denies the fact that they were spoken. The secretary of the Commission who signs the communication knows that they are untrue because he was present at the time they were spoken. The members of the F. U. M. Commission know they are untrue because they were present when he uttered these words. And he said more that night — "If others can do illegal and immoral things, you can." And he said even more. He became enraged and when I was attempting to develop my continued objection to the granting of the loans, he stopped me bruskly and said that I need not talk any more and that I could do what I pleased. This, after I had allowed him at previous meetings and at that meeting to talk as long as he pleased in spite of the fact that his talk unquestionably would have irritated an angel. —and I am by no means an angel. But I tried during my whole time in the Order Sons of Italy to avoid personal rows, personal offenses and personal crimination and recrimination. I tried to put all the matters up for discussion on a more elevated plane than the plane of personality—upon the plane of ideas. But they would not have it so. This man thought — and reacted to the thought — that I was objecting to the granting of the loan because of some objection to him. But what an absurdity. Anybody who knows me knows that I do not make objections upon personal grounds even in the case of persons whom I dislike. And in this case it was perfectly patent that my objection was to the thing itself, since I was opposing my ideas to the ideas of men in the Order, the Grand Council and the F. U. M. Commission against whom nobody ever dreamed I had any rancor or dislike.

He stopped me and naturally I felt the resentment of a man as well as the reaction of a presiding officer. That was too much. To allow a man like him even to come within the limits of the Commission was to honor him sufficiently Yet he not only comes there and argues a proposal against the wishes and the opinion of the presiding officer but he actually tells the presiding officer to shut up and to do what he pleases. I told him that he did not have any right to speak or act in that way; that I was the presiding officer and had a right to express my views even to a fuller extent than anybody else had expressed his views. He came forward, approached me, came right close to me and shaking his hand in my face said: "You think you are intelligent. You'll see. I'll fix you." He was the dominant man of the Order. He was the God of the machine. He could make and unmake men. And so he would show how easily he could destroy me. I certainly would have been destroyed—but not by him—asall men are degraded and destroyed who stay in the Order long enough—if I had stayed in longer.

That man very little knows my desires and ambitions in this world and his influence upon those desires and ambitions. Let him know —I state it openly that he may use his influence to prevent the consummation of the ambition of my life: I desire to become President of the United States!

The communication says: "Whoever knows Counselor Miele knows by long experience that he is too clever to deliver himself into the hands of Ferrari by uttering words which are so compromising." Ah! But the cleverest are sometimes the stupidest. He can call, according to his henchmen, spirits from the vasty deep. But he is not as they call me, a metaphysician. He is a practical man. I know a trick worth two of his. When a man's object is frustrated he becomes as mad as a march hare—as Miele was raving mad that night. Anybody can be clever in baseness. To be clever in the higher regions of thought and action is the prize of life. Certainly this Miele doesn't even know by remotest acquaintance those higher regions of thought and action.

The officers of the Mourtuary Fund and the Grand Council could not have acted in good faith. My objections began immediately upon the presentation of the proposal for a loan of $2500 on the 14th of December 1925. My objections were elaborated at great length and were summarized in a letter I wrote to the Commission on the 11th day of January 1926.

Just as soon as doubts concerning the validity of the loan by the Mortuary Fund were raised it was their duty to seek out the opinion of the Law Committee or of Counsel, or the attorneys in the pending case. This they did not do in spite or repeated objections made by me, to the Grand Venerable, to members of the Grand Council, to members of the F. U. M. and to numerous brothers of the Order, begun on the 14th day of December 1925, and continued until the very end. It was only after these repeated objections that on the 15th day of January 1926, the Grand Venerable, as the result of my objections and my expositions of those objections to him personally, as well as to him as a member of groups to whom I had talked, went to one of the lawyers in the case and asked him for an opinion. I do not know personally of the consultation of the Grand Venerable with the attorney. I know of it only through the fact that he told it before the combined meeting on the night of January 15th.

But even if from the beginning they had shown good faith and immediately upon objection raised, particularly when the objection came not only from a lawyer of the Law Committee but from counsel to the Grand Lodge, and President of the Mortuary Fund, from which the loan was to be taken, if there is any breach of morals or of law, the Grand Council and the Mortuary Fund cannot find protection in the invalid opinion of an attorney. An attorney's opinion is given for what it is worth; it cannot change the law. That law is applied to the individual breaking it without regard to professional opinion rendered. The opinion, however, may be taken as an extenuating circumstance by the judge who passes sentence.

When the question was presented to the attorney by the Grand Venerable, it had two phases, that of a loan by the Mortuary Fund of $2500 for the payment of attorneys fees and that of a loan of $1700 for the payment of the expenses of the Grand Delegates. The oral opinion—and it is to be understood that in no case did they produce a written opinion of an attorney—decided in favor of the loan of $2500 and against the loan of $1700. What distinction of principle there is between one loan and the other I do not know and I should be willing to give a prize to any one who could tell me that distinction.

The By-Laws of the Mortuary Fund read as follows:

"Article I.—The Grand Lodge of the State of New York by resolution passed at the meeting of the 23rd of May, 1915, establishes the Mortuary Fund in order that brothers may reciprocally help one another in misfortune. The benefits of the Mortuary Fund represent an act of benevolence toward a brother or his family in misfortune."

The purposes therefore for which the Mortuary Fund was established, are perfectly clear. It does not need a Philadelphia lawyer to interpret the meaning of Article I. The purpose of the Mortuary Fund is not to grant loans or to invest in loans to and adventures of the Grand Council or the Supreme Council, but it is representative and manifestative of the benevolent acts which brothers of the Order do to one another in time of misfortune. It is to be used, in other words, for death benefits to help the family of the dead brother with.

Article 36 speaks of monthly contributions. These monthly contributions are made by members of the Order for death benefits, not for loans by the Mortuary Fund. It is ridiculous to suppose that these monthly contributions for death benefits could be risked, as in this case, by lending without security—for the payment of attorneys' fees.

The New York rule on trust funds is clear and decisive. The money turned into the Mortuary Fund is a trust fund, to be used only for the specific purposes indicated by the law of the Mortuary Fund and imposed by the general law of the land. In this case, it is particularly clear that it is a trust fund and that it is to be considered as an especially sacred trust fund. First, because it is a death benefit fund;

secondly, because in this case, you have the general law of New York State and the general principles of law operating to make an appropria- tion of those funds to any except specific death benefits, an irregular proceding and unwarranted by the law; thirdly, because of a crucial fact which I presented to the Grand Council and which was discussed by the Grand Council on the 15th day of January namely: that the Grand Convention at Schenectady in August 1925, had authorized the raising of an emergency Mortuary Fund by the loan of one dollar by each member of any Lodge which desired to contribute to the formation of an emergency Mortuary Fund.

This, to take up the last three points in inverse order, was a clear expression of opinion upon the part of the Grand Lodge of the pur- pose for which the loan contributions of one dollar were to be used by the Mortuary Commission. At the January 15th meeting, which I have mentioned, the Grand Venerable and others thought that you could make a division of the moneys in the Mortuary Fund into moneys loaned at the rate of one dollar a member of a Lodge, and monthly contributions made by the Lodges to the Mortuary Fund; and that the loan of $2500 for the payment of attorneys' fees could properly be made from the $1 loan contributions in the Mortuary Fund. This argument I also combatted and told them that I, as President could not vote in favor of the granting of a loan from either the loan con- tributions or the monthly contributions to the Mortuary Fund.

The law of the State of New York is express and strict in the obligations it imposes upon the trustee. The State provides that a trustee may invest in bond and mortgages on unencumbered real pro- perty within the State, or Government bond or obligations, and to a limited extent in certain Railway bonds. (Decedent Estate Law Sec. 111 (1909) Amend. Laws 1918 c. 544, Sec. 1; Laws 1922, c.593 Banking Laws Sec. 239; (1914) Amend. Laws 1918, c. 270, Sec. 1 Laws 1925, c. 107). — Columbia Law Review April 1926.

It is evident then, that the law of the State of New York allows the investment of trust funds only in the specified instances mention ed in the Statute.

But it needs no ghost come from the grave to tell us that. Aside from the State law, the making of a loan by the Mortuary Fund with money which was given to be used for the specific purpose of paying death benefits with, cannot be used to lend to a body within the Order Sons of Italy or outside the Order Sons of Italy, in order that this body may pay a fee to attorneys in pending litigation. Common sense and the common decencies of life both forbid.

The communication says, "Ferrari had, because of the position he occupied, many attestations of sympathy, the last attestation that of a bouquet of fresh flowers on the occasion of the New Year's Day meeting held at the offices of the Order." See, gentlemen of the public, they tried to influence me with fresh flowers. I must be some- thing either subhuman or superhuman to resist even the fragrance of fresh flowers given on New Year's Day!

> That glib and oily art,
> To speak and purpose not.—Shakespeare.

Self defense is nature's eldest law.—Dryden.

The letter of the Mortuary Commission of April 26, 1926, denies that there are any falsities, or any inexactnesses or inaccuracies in the minutes, and says that these minutes contain the development of the subject during the discussion and the resolutions adopted.

On Jan. 11, 1926, as the result of my reading the minutes of the meeting of Dec. 14, 1925, a reading which had occurred so long after the meeting of Dec. 14th because of the fact that they had been sent to me only on the 11th of January, I wrote the following letter to the Secretary of the Commission, complaining of the inaccuracy of the minutes.

Mr. Mario De Pasquale,   January 11, 1926.

Secretary Mortuary Fund, 27 Cleveland Place, New York City.

Dear Brother De Pasquale:

I have looked over the minutes of the last meeting of the F. U. M. Commission.

You deal fully with the discussion upon all points not only in these minutes but in the minutes that have gone before. However, upon the most important matter that has come before the Commission you say only a few words and the report is extremely inaccurate as well as lacking in detail. The matter I refer to is the question of the loan of $2,500 to be made by the F. U. M. to the Grand Council of the Order in our State for the payment of a retainer to the attorneys in the case. The question of the loan was presented to the Commission by Brother Stephen Miele. After his presentation of that question before the Commission I asked the opinion of all the Commissioners as to the advisability of granting the loan. The Commissioners one after the other answered me that they saw no objection. After I had gotten the opinion of everybody on the Commission I spoke at length giving my reasons for my opposition to the granting of the loan.

I said first that the Commission as it was, representing only the New York members, did not have legal power to pass upon such an important question. The whole Committee should have been summoned. Secondly, I doubted the legal power of even the full Commission to grant the loan. Thirdly, I doubted the moral correctness of granting that loan because of the peculiar circumstances under which the money had been confided to the care of the F. U. M. It seemed to me to be a trust fund which we cannot risk. Fourthly, it seemed highly improper for me as President of the F. U. M., and as counsel to the Grand Lodge to lend money to the Grand Council which was for the payment of a retainer to the attorneys of the Council. It was like taking money out of the treasury of the F. U. M., to put it into my pocket.

The Commission finally agreed to let the matter go over, and upon my request gave me power to call the Commission together for the discussion of that question any time I might consider it fitting; further that I was going to make an investigation of the various problems involved and that upon the basis of that investigation I was to make up my mind what to do concerning the calling together of the Commission again.

I did make the investigation and I spoke to you about the result of my deliberations in the presence of the Treasurer and the Assistant Scretary. I told you that I had decided permanently against the granting of the loan.

There was therefore no necessity of putting the matter on the order of business for the next meeting.

In addition the report lacks a statement which ought to be made, namely how the question was brought before the Commission. The matter was presented to the Commission by Brother Stephen Miele who gave his reasons for the granting of the loan.

On the question of the Italian Hospital, the report in the minutes also does not state that Brother Stephen Miele was the man that presented that question to the Commission. The minutes are inexact in that they say that I made a strong recommendation for the giving of the $200.00 to the Italian Hospital. Under the peculiar circumstances of the case and of that night I decline to have the minutes state what did not occur, namely, that I strongly recommended the proposal. After asking each of the Commission for his opinion I just simply concurred by silence.

The minutes ought to state that the matter of the $200.00 to the Italian Hospital was presented to the Commission by Brother Miele. The implication in the minutes is that I presented the matter myself since the opening statement speaks of the recommendation made by me.

RF/RN   Cordially and fraternally yours,

But before the meeting of Dec. 14th, I had complained of the inaccuracy of the minutes to the secretary and after the meeting of Dec. 14th I wrote the letter which follows, to the Secretary.

Mr. Trapani,   December 18, 1925.

c/o Order Sons of Italy, 27 Cleveland Place, New York City.

Dear Trapani:

Will you be good enough to come to see me and show me all bills and circulars and letters written by members of the Commission or employees, for the past month and a half.

RF/RJ   Cordially and fraternally yours,

The M. F. in the letter of April 26, says that I should have made my objections. These letters show conclusively that I did object right along but that in spite of repeated objections the minutes continued to be inaccurate.

The letter says that I should have objected to the payment of expenditures which had not been authorized by the Commission instead of waitng until after the event and having hindsight rather than foresight. I did complain at the time, on the 14th of December when the expenses which we had not authorized, were presented to us for payment upon the recommendation of the Grand Council, which paid half the bill and desired us to pay the other half and the last paragraph of letter of Dec. 18th, 1925, if poof. (See page 61 for letter).

They say that my failure to object is an indication of my non-curancy and thoughtfulness.

The letter which I have just published destroys that illusion.

To show that even from the beginning I was careful in my dealings with the Commission and desired to be informed concerning everything that happened and the care I took to keep abreast, I publish this letter of August 31, 1925, to the Assistant Secretary.

Mr. F. Trapani,   August 31, 1925.
Assistant Secretary, Order Sons of Italy, 27 Cleveland Place, New York.
Dear Brother Trapani:

Thank you for the report of the State of the Mortuary Fund.
It gives me a very good idea of what has been done.
Please send me a note every day of the state of the fund and the happenings of the office.
Many thanks!
RF/RJ   Sincerely yours,

They say that I desired to raise a spirit of hate against the men who directed the Order. I do not know anything of hate and the only hate I have ever known was the hate that I saw rampant and flaming in the Order itself.
On Oct. 8, 1925, I wrote a letter which was published in all Italian newspapers down State and up State, which sets forth the rights of combatants and neutrals and I tried to keep balance and poise instead of running off into an abyss of hate.

Editor of Corriere D'America,   October 8, 1925.
309 Lafayette Street, New York City.
Dear Editor:

I am very grateful to you for having published my communication in today's issue.
The rank and file of the members of the Order ought not to be made to suffer when they have had no part in the grave consequences of the Schism.
RF/RJ

On the 4th of November, 1925, I wrote to the Assistant Secretary, complaining of a communication which had gone out of the office without my knowledge and telling him in the absence of the Secretary, that I did not like a paragraph which used strong and filthy language directed against our adversaries.

Mr. Trapani,   November 4, 1925.
Order Sons of Italy, 27 Cleveland Place, New York City.
Dear Trapani:

Will you be good enough to show me all material intended for publication.
I do not like the 5th full paragraph in the second column of the Corriere this morning, of your communication to the press from the F. U. M.
Mr. De Pasquale is out of town at present. Will you be good enough to tell him I should like to speak with him when he comes back.

RF/RJ   Sincerely yours,

This is the first and only communication that went out of the office of the Mortuary Commission without my consent or knowledge, except the first communication to the Press, which was not written by me but by the Secretary, but which, however, I read before its being sent out.

I was not interested in hating individuals but in establishing the principles upon which the Order could move to noble heights. I was interested in the question as to whether any group had a right to secede from the Order. I was interested in the question of the powers of the Supreme Council and of the Grand Councils. I was interested in the question of State autonomy.

They advise me to have resigned a week before I did, namely on the 27th day of Jan., 1926, and in this way I could have avoided signing the check. I have expounded at length, in a different portion of this narration, the reasons which led me to wait until after the Washington Convention and the reasons why I thought it advisable to let the matter come to a vote. Here I shall say only this.

On the 15th of January, at the combined meeting of the Grand Council and the M. F. which was to recommend a loan of $2,500 to the M. F. the minutes of that meeting did not show that the recommendation was made. The meeting of the M. F. of January 22nd called for the purpose of acting upon the recommendation, if any had been made, by the G. C. did not so act because no such recommendation appeared in the G. C. minutes, of that evening, written up by the acting Secretary of the G. C.

It would have been a cowardly act upon my part at this juncture of affairs to leave the Commission. It was contended, and with force, that a mistake had been made in the minutes. The manly thing to do was to give them an opportunity of correcting the mistake. And yet it was not proper for the Commission to act at the meeting of January 22nd. There had to be another meeting—the meeting of January 29th for the purpose of voting upon the recommendation of the Grand Council, if any recommendation were presented. That recommendation came and it was the duty of the President to put the matter to a vote.

Furthermore, these men who now advise resigning under cowardly circumstances, are the very men who were howling murder and predicting the immediate destruction of the whole Order, if one of two things happened; either I did not bring the matter of a loan of $2,500 to a vote in the Commission or I resigned, or both. Their gratitude is prodigious.

However, on the 28th day of January, 1926, one day before the meeting at which the Commission was to vote upon the loan of $2,500 I did express the desire to resign in a letter to the Grand Venerable. (See page 26). The expression of a desire to resign, if accepted, would not have been the cowardly act that it would have been if I had decided without consultation to give up the men and the fight to the maws of gaping time.

These people accuse me of hypersensibility. But see how I

had to treat even the so-called old diplomat and old fox of the Order, the Secretary of the M. F. At a meeting at the beginning of October, or end of September of the Grand Council, and representatives of Mortuary Commission and Supreme Council I had had occasion to praise the work of the acting secretary to the Grand Council. The old fox of the Order wrote me a long letter, telling me that I injured his dignity because I praised the acting secretary of the Grand Council. I had to treat him and the rest of them just like a lot of children. See how I humored him as Hamlet humors Polonious, in the letter I wrote him on the 6th of October, 1925.

Mr. Mario De Pasquale,   October 6, 1925.

Secretary Mortuary Fund, 27 Cleveland Place, New York City.

Dear Mr. De Pasquale:

You misunderstood completely my remarks at the Grand Council meeting on Friday night. I am perfectly certain that you were the only one who did misunderstand. Praise of one is not dispraise of another. Because the occasion demanded praise of another person, that praise did not mean disparagement of your work. Whe nthe occasion arises I shall be very glad to testify to the quality of your work.

But since you have brought up in your letter the desire for consultation between us, pray, why did you make your report to the Grand Council without going over the matter with me or at least informing me that the report was to be made.

These are all small things and we should not be irritated by them. Let's be generous and large-minded and try to adjust ourselves to one another. I am certain that we shall have a complete adjustment in a short time. The slight friction that has arisen is due to the novelty of our acquaintance. This will soon wear off.

I should like to talk over the business of the meeting of October 10th. Kindly see me on Thursday if you are in town then.

RF/RJ   Sincerely yours,

They tell you that I declined to sign many important and urgent administrative papers. So far as death benefits are concerned the only two cases which I temporarily objected to, because of the insufficiency of the papers submitted to us, according to the law of the M. F. were these mentioned in a letter of November 6, 1925.

They say I desire to cause a revolution in their ranks. If I had wanted to cause a revolution at the time of my resignation I could have given the reasons for my resignation—reasons which I gave in my statement to the Press and in the interviews to E. Valentini. Instead, my letters of resignation both to the Grand Venerable and to the Venerable of my Subordinate Lodge are devoid of any reasons for my withdrawal. Yet, these people have the branzen-facedness to accuse me of not having given reasons for my resignation. If they say that these reasons were given two months afterwards I reply, that even before the

Washington Convention I indicated some of the reasons to the Grand Venerable in the letter of January 28th.

They tell you that it was necessary to get a loan from the Mortuary Commission. These people will stop at nothing and they have absolutely no shame. They will assume a bad position and argue from that position to the crack of doom without winking an eye.

The granting of the loan was from every conceivable point of view an erroneous thing. These reasons I have indicated in another portion of this narration. I had told them that instead of coming to the Commission they could ask for authorization, to take the money from the Commission's fund, from the individuals and the lodges that had lent the money to the M. F. or they could get a new loan from the subordinate lodges. A few dollars from each would have made up the whole amount, or they could have gotten a few more people in the Order who would contribute a certain amount and make up the $2,500. At the meeting of January 12, 1926, I made the suggestion that I was willing to put in my share if a few people got together for the purpose of gathering the money. But no, none of these methods was feasible, according to them. It was most easy and most convenient to come to the Commission and put their hands into the Treasury and let the Members of the Commission take the primary responsibility.

The minutes of the Grand Council, meeting of January 15, 1926, read as follows:

The Grand Venerable Freschi explains the reasons for the meeting that is, "to provide necessary means for the payment of the expenses of the Supreme Delegates to the Supreme Convention of Washington, D. C., and of the expenses of the case against the Sons of Italy Grand Lodge." He says that the following states have expressed a desire to contribute to the expenses of the case—the States of Pennsylvania, Connecticut and New Jersey; and that the Grand Council of the State of New York has obligated itself to give a loan of $2,500, which loan is to be made by the F. U. M.

"The question has already been presented to the Commission and its President Counsellor Ferrari has declared himself contrary to a loan, to be made by the F. U .M.; the money of the M. F. being a trust fund and therefore not to be touched" * * *

"A recommendation is made to the M. F. to set aside the part of the fund lent by the Subordinate Lodges in order that it may be ready if and when these Subordinate Lodges desire the restitution of their loans. Approved."

The minutes of January 15, 1926, contain no recommendation to the M. F. to grant the loan of $2,500. These minutes contain only the recommendation concerning the division of the funds into loan and monthly contribution funds. It was their intention after repeated objections and discussion upon my part, in the presence of the combined meeting and out of the combined meeting, before it and after it, to make an eleventh hour attempt to do what I had been telling them to do for over a month, namely, to get authorization from the Subordinate Lodges that had made loan contributions to the fund, to lend the money to the Grand Council for the purpose of paying the attorneys.

I therefore, could not put to a vote, in spite of uproarious proceedings on the part of one of the Miele clan, who is on the Commission, the question of the granting of the loan. That had to go over for another meeting.

I called for the 22nd day of January, a meeting of the whole Commission down State and up State, and I indicated in a letter to the Acting Grand Secretary, that no representative of the Grand Council, other than the Grand Venerable, should come to the Mortuary Commission to give the reasons for the recommendation to make the loan in opposition to my objection to it. It was only fair that I invite some man opposed to my own ideas, in order to argue the case against me. This is the letter, Jan. 19, 1926:

> "Dear Frank: I think the whole Commission should be notified—out of town as well as New York City Commissioners. Do it by telegram.
>
> I think Freschi ought to come to the meeting. **No** other representative of the Grand Council.
>
> Cordially yours,
>
> "BOB."

At the meeting of January 15, 1926, there were present: Six members of the Grand Council, the acting secretary of the Grand Council, who had no vote, and Stephen Miele, the representative of the Supreme Council, who had no vote.

There were two members from down State absent and all the three members from up State were absent.

Of the Mortuary Commission there were present, five: Two were absent. Both M. F. and Grand Council members absent from down State, had expressed their approval of the loan of $2,500.

CHAPTER IV.

FALL OF THE ACTION

and

DENOUMENT

The Meeting of the Grand Delegates at my Office in February, 1926.

Even if I had acted tyranically I should have been justified because the rottenness of officials of the Order was so great that a cleaning out of the Augean Stables was the work of prime and pressing importance.

"In his soul, however, in which there was nourished the most profound hatred of the men who could not allow him to realize his Utopia of wishing to destroy the constituted authorities, and substitute himself for them he was harboring the most ferocious vendetta against them, and commenced, immediately after leaving the order, a campaign of insinuation, of underground voices and of secret interviews given to our adversaries, which culminated in the publication of a communcation to the press under his name and of an interview in which he made the most atrocious statements to our injury, in the hope of producing a revolution in our ranks and in the ranks of those who have remained faithful to the Order Sons of Italy in America and who have sworn to support its ranks." Thus circular No. 21.

Since my resignation and up to the time of the communication by F. U. M. to the press on the 29th day of March, 1926, I was as silent and as mysterious as the sphinx of old. I did not even discuss the matter with my most intimate friends. It is true I was importuned to speak. It is true I was urged by acquaintances and friends to say what I knew but I preferred to follow my own course. Indeed I was so nauseated with men and events that for some days I was incapable of speaking about the Order without complete revulsion. It was in this state of mind that I declined to receive a Committee of the Grand Council who desired to see me to urge me to withdraw my resignation. I thought their coming would be of no use; I had made up my mind and I did not want to talk about the subject any longer. I wanted to be left in peace, the men in the Order could fight it out among themselves. There were enough men in the Order who knew why I left to make a good big fight within the ranks of the Order without my contributing anything to the combat. So it was that I wrote the following letter to Mr. Panetta, who, as acting Secretary of the Grand Council had phoned me in my absence and left a message asking me to receive a Committee of the Grand Council to urge me to withdraw my letter of resignation. (See letter in Appendix 3).

Several weeks after when my mind had settled to an even tenor and I was able to look at men and events of the Order without passion, with cold reason and philosophical calm, Mr. Capparelli, Editor of the Nuovo Vesillo called me up on the 'phone and asked me to meet a committee. I did not desire to hurt Mr. Capperelli, but I avoided the interview as best I could. I avoided the interview for a whole week and I then consented, upon his insistence, and upon the insistence of many Grand Delegates, to receive the Committee with Capparelli at its head. A few days before the Committee came to see me there dropped into my office unexpectedly, two men, Mr. Lorrello and Mr. Sidoti, to whom I spoke for over an hour and to whom I related the most salient facts concerning my resignation. Another day, Mr. Iannone, a member of the Grand Council came in to see me, who urged me to withdraw my resignation and to whom I said I could not and told him in a very few words why, although that was not necessary inasmuch as he knew all about the loans and the interference of Miele in the affairs of the F. U. M.

The Committee of 15 Grand Delegates with Mr. Capparelli at its head, came to my office and were there from 5 until 9 P. M. I must have spoken at least 3 hours during the four hours they were here and for the first two hours at least, I was able to give them a full and detailed narrative of the events that led to my resignation. They were put in complete possession of the most important facts in the case. It was necessary for me to do this because, although I had explained the difficulties I was having to the Grand Venerable Freschi, Angrisani, one of the members of the Grand Council and Panetta, the acting Secretary of the Grand Council, at a meeting which I shall describe in a moment, I desired Grand Delegates and members of the Order, who were not officially connected with the administration to know why I had taken the stand I did because, inasmuch as I had left the Order, I should not have been in a position to debate the question on the floor of the Convention, when that Convention was held. I wanted to justify myself to myself and to men whom I respected, members of the Order. It was my duty to present the facts to them, as it was their duty, if they found those facts to be true to produce within the order a revolution, by the cutting off of official and unofficial heads, particularly the unofficial heads, who without responsibility, were exercising all the privileges and the advantages of power.

I particularly spoke to these men of the nefarious work done by the evil spirit of the Order, the hoodoo and the Jonah— Stephen Miele. I related to them from first to last, everything that man had done to try to win me over and when he found he could not win me over by blandishment, taffy and salve, everything that he had done to crush me. Not only that, he had attempted, I explained to these people, not only to put me in a compromising position with respect to the members of the Order and to the world outside, but also to cause the ruin of the members of the Mortuary Fund and the members of the Grand Council, who were unconscious instruments, perhaps, of his, or who did not at least, understand the full meaning of the consequences of their acts; and to cause the ruin of the Order itself. He wanted to lay hands on the Mortuary Fund; and he insisted upon this time after time, in season and out of season, in the Commission and out, in the Grand Council and out of the Grand Council. It was necessary, he said, indeed vital, to the health and the life of the Order, that the M. F. should grant a loan of $2,500 to the Grand Council for the payment of attorney's fees; and $1,700 for the payment of the expenses of Grand Delegates, who were going to Washington.

It was a ruinous proceeding, ruinous from every possible point of view. The Schenectady group was asking in an equity proceeding, for an accounting of the funds of the Sons of Italy Grand Lodge by the officers of that Lodge. With what grace could the Schenectady group go into Court and demand that accounting of the Sons of Italy Grand Lodge. Our group wanted to know what the other side had done with the funds of the Order. Would it not have been a crushing reply for the other side to have demanded an accounting of the funds in our group. In a court of equity the complainant should come into Court with clean hands. If his hands are soiled, no matter how besmirched the other party is, a Court of Equity will not take into consideration the prayers made by the complainant. And even if this matter would not have been brought up, even assuming—a matter beyond the reach of imagination—that the other side would not take advantage of such a highly advantageous situation for them, and desperate situation for us, it was a matter which could at any time in the future have been brought up by the other side, or by a member of our own group, not only as a moral question but also as a legal one.

I told these men I had been opposed to the loan of $2,500 and that of $1,700. I had been opposed to them from the beginning and remained opposed until the very end. They knew when they were in Washington with me, that the loan of $2,500 had been voted by the Mortuary Fund and that I had voted in the negative—my vote being the only adverse vote. They were in caucus and heard the Grand Venerable Freschi say that they had the check to be presented to the Supreme Council and that the members of the Commission had voted according to their lights, the reference being to me who had voted against the granting of the loan. I told these delegates I had prevented a vote upon the question of a loan for over a month and a half. I went farther and said I could possibly have prevented a vote longer until after the Washington Convention if I had desired but that I felt it a moral responsibility inasmuch as the unanimous current of opinion was against me to put the matter to a vote and let the majority decide upon the policy of the F. U. M. and the Grand Council and let that majority take the responsibility before the Grand Lodge and the Order. I told these men that I made desperate efforts in order to save their skins; that I made desperate efforts not only to save the skins of the officers but to save the face of the Order. I had my mind bent not only upon today or tomorrow, but the day after tomorrow; upon next year and the year after that. Chickens will come home to roost and the officers of today would be called to account, although temporarily, they were exercising plenary authority and plenary power and were riding rough shod over all the decencies of life, as well as the legalities and the moralities. They were like a locomotive without an engineer, which was crashing and thundering to the abyss.

It was my duty, I told these Grand Delegates, to do what I could to prevent the diving of the officers into the chasm, but unfortunately they had no wills of their own. The Grand Officers and Commissioners of the F. U. M. either did not see the near or remote consequences of their acts, or were being driven by a will superior to their own, the will of Stephen Miele and the Supreme Officers of the Order Sons of Italy in America. For, be it understood, the Supreme Officers had thought it perfectly justifiable to obtain the loan out of the Mortuary Fund. One of the States, it was being said, had already given a loan to their Grand Council for the payment of these attorneys' fees out of the treasury of the M. F. Why could not New York, that was particularly and most vitally interested in the outcome of the litigation.

I said that it was impossible to do any business in the M. F. while Miele was around. He obstructed the work of the commission in every way, he made proposals which were not acceptable and continued to make the proposals in spite of the irritation his persistence caused. I told these men we did not require any advice. That we had sufficient intelligence and learning and power of decision to deliberate and decide questions for ourselves. I told them that I had gone to the Grand Venerable and presented the constant interference of this man and had told the Grand Venerable, that either Miele would have to be eliminated or I would eliminate myself. The Grand Venerable was of the opinion that he ought not to come before the Commission if I did not desire him to. From the moment that question was decided, Miele never appeared before the commission again. At the combined meeting, of which I shall soon speak, of the Grand Council and the Mortuary Fund, held on the 15th day of January, 1926, I took the Grand Venerable Freschi, Panetta and Angrisani aside and explained to them in detail what had occurred at a previous meeting, which I have designated as the critical or crisis meeting. At this critical meeting (see Chap. III) held on the 12th day of January, 1926, Miele had decided to force a decision in his favor, of the Commission on the granting of the loan, and because I continued to be against it he became enraged and abused everybody and everything, me included. He made statements, which I told the Delegates which show there was no common ground between him and me, and that is was impossible, if the members of the Fund and the Grand Council supported him, for me to retain my connection with the Fund or the Order itself.

But what I wanted was that the Delegates be perfectly clear in their minds on one solid, substantial, ineradicable fact, and that was this. That although what happened at the critical meeting of January 12, 1926, was sufficient reason for any member's resigning and leaving the M. F. into the hands of other people who would do Miele's bidding and who fell in with the general current of opinion, the Delegates must not understand that was the only cause operating to produce my state of mind in resigning. There was a long series of events preceding that meeting, that had determined me to leave as soon as I could honorably do so.

I was surrounded by obstacles. The most elementary things pertaining to the administration of the Order I could not do or have done. I could not bear the constant, everlasting and unfathomable hate in which I had to do my work. It was an atmosphere and an environment of inordinate, profound and venomous rancor toward individuals. There was never any discussion of ideas, never any discussion of the ideals of the Order or of the aims of the Italians in this country, and the methods of reaching those aims. It was only how to destroy this man on the other side and that man. It was an atmosphere stifling, choking and crushing. The atmosphere was so thick and heavy, pressing down upon the individuals of the Order, especially those at the top, that either a person immediately became impressed and stamped with the imprint of hate toward individuals or he revolted and got out of the influence of it.

I told them that there was dominant in the order, not only in the State of New York, but in Washington, at the National Convention, the same Miele whose elimination I had demanded from the M. F. meetings; that that domination was debasing to the Order and debasing to the individuals who allowed it; and that his influence was particularly nefarious because of the fact that he had no office in the Grand Lodge and was constantly exerting pressure upon the officers of the Grand Lodge. I said that his influence ought to be eradicated immediately, because it was a degrading influence. If his direction had been intelligent and elevating, even though he held no position and exerted authority and even domination, we might have partly excused the benevolent despotism. But in his case, there was neither intelligence nor elevation. His schemes did not tend to make the Order rise to the mountain tops; they tended rather to make it sink to the ocean depths. Anybody has the cleverness to do base and ignoble things; but to do thing of nobility requires the highest intelligence and the highest character. He was on the job all the time and his family was on the job and his clan was on the job and it was impossible for anybody to fight them unless he too was constantly on the front line of combat. I was not in a position to take that front place of combat. I had my own work, I had my own living to make and I did not live as Stephen Miele did, upon the Order. He was bone of its bone and flesh of its flesh. I had to make my living outside; and further, there are certain things gentlemen will not do, even though they lose a fight by not doing them. There are certain base depths to which gentlemen do not descend, even though in refusing to descend to those depths, they may lose what certain persons would consider prizes of life. In order to combat him it was necessary to use his own means and those means I would not stoop to .

There should be a propaganda of enlightenment among the masses of the Order; a propaganda of enlightenment which would illuminate the minds of the masses and make them hurl from their pedestals these gods with feet of clay, who make sport of the most sacred things belonging to the Italians of the United States, namely, their good name and their honor. For this propaganda I had not the sufficient time. It was the business of those who knew the conditions of the Order—the business of not only one individual but a squadron. If the Delegates cared for me as much as they professed to care for me, if they respected me as highly as they said they did, if they thought my loss to the Order was a great loss, it was their duty to prevent a similar loss in the future, a loss which would inevitably recur just so long as he and men like him retained unlimited and irresponsible control. The legacy that I could leave to them was an exposition of the facts that had driven me out—a heritage priceless enough if the Grand Delegates would make the proper use of it. My loss was the loss of one individual and tomorrow another would come and take my place. They were too flattering in telling me that I was irreplaceable. They exalted me too much in saying that they wanted men like me to be the directors and the guiding spirits of the Order. A long series of events had made it impossible for me to remain any longer. I had taken my decision and my decision was irrevocable. I thought rapidly and acted rapidly and although my decisions might appear to the unobservant and unintelligent world to be the result of impulses because they came so swiftly, they must know that my decisions were not on impulse and on the spur of the moment but deliberative—only the deliberation was swft.

They must, however, know the facts because they themselves had been kept in the dark concerning what had happened in the Commission and what the dominating gang had tried to do to me to bend me to their will, in order that they might have within their hands proper weapons with which to fight the opposition.

It was impossible because of the presence within the Commission and within the Order itself, of Stephen Miele, to discuss questions with freedom. Opposition to his ideas was considered personal opposition to him. If you debated a proposal he presented he thought it was a personal injury done to him. It did not matter how kindly and gently you presented your own ideas, there was nothing that could satisfy him except a complete subjugation to his desires. In such an atmosphere it was of course, impossible to work. The members of the Mortuary Commission were indeed, courteous, respectful and admiring of their President. But it was dolorous just the same to see how the Members of the Commission were of his opinion almost all the time without argument presented. It was fortunate for me to have such an ascendency over the members of the Commission otherwise, the vote upon the loan for $2,500 would have taken place immediately. I postponed and adjourned, and adjourned and postponed until it was no longer possible on account of the number of meetings we had had, to postpone any longer. I tried to analyze the psychology of the Members of the Commission; I tried to discover their motives; I tried to delve into the reasons, secret and patent, of the dominance of this individual over them, and I found that dominance for the most part to lie in the fact, that they thought he was a "Deus Ex Machina," a god of the machine who could work miracles because he had been a Grand Venerable and a Supreme Venerable in the Order Sons of Italy in America and was a veteran in all the underground processes such a man is heir to. He had a further hold upon them in that at the Schenectady Convention, he, as the representative of the Supreme Council and as one who had taken an active part in that Convention, was the cause of their nomination. Without his consent my nomination too would probably not have been possible. Indeed it was he who, after I declined to accept the position of Grand Orator, and declined to him and to others the position of president of the M. F. finally said to me that they wanted me as President of the M. F. for the prestige of my name. Since the members of the M. F. were his creatures, why should they not do his will. It was requiring a great deal of human nature to demand of the Members of the Mortuary Commission to stand upon their own feet. I thought the upstate members were more independent of the influence of this man; and at the beginning they seemed to be, but I soon found out that his round-about and underground methods reached even the up-State Delegates and although these delegates respected and admired me, even more, if possible, than the down-State Delegates, they too, on the critical occasion, veered round from a position in favor of my negative vote on the granting of the loan to a position in accord with the wishes of the Grand Mogul.

His desire to dominate everything and to have his fingers in every pie, indeed his every finger in every pie, is shown even in this. He was elected honorary member of the M. F. upon the proposal of the Secretary of the M. F. and a very short time after that, new letterheads of the M. F. appeared with his name heading the list of officers of the M. F. and with the significant and distinguished title of Honorary President.

My friends, who are now my enemies, upon the M. F.—because now they have given out to the world the famous communication to the press, published in The Corriere of April 26, 1926, in which they all say that the various things I have charged the M. F. with never occurred, in which they say that my charge that the M. F. Minutes are mutilated and false, is not true, and that the various things which happened at the critical meeting did not happen—these will now unquestionably deny the fact, as they do in this letter of April 26th, will probably deny this either outright or try to throw a smoke-screen about the whole affair as they do in the communication to the press of April 26th, concerning what I say about Miele's honorary membership. I never said that he was anything but an honorary member. I never said he was an Honorary President, as the communication makes me out to say. I said in a previous communication to the press what I say now, that although an honorary member, he became transformed and transfigured into an honorary President upon the letter heads a few days after election as honorary member. Who was the guardian spirit that traced in letters of gold upon the letterheads of the Order Sons of Italy the name of

Avv. Cav. S. Miele
as Honorary President?

Circular No. 15 of the Grand Lodge of the State of New York, dated January 5, 1925 (a misprint for 1926) shows in full and flowing uniform these precious words

"Presidente Onorario
Avv. Cav. S. Miele"

I said nothing about this because the matter seemed to be so absolutely absurd and idiotic upon its face and so symptomatic and representative of the individual who had had it done. At the combined meeting of the Grand Council and M. F. on the 15th of January, when I spoke to Freschi, Panetta and Angrisani about the meeting of the 12th of January, I spoke of this incident, insignificant it is perfectly true, yet highly revelatory.

Circular No. 17 issued February 10, 1926, eliminated, upon the insistence of Panetta with the consent of the Grand Venerable, the name and the pompous title of the Chevalier.

I told the Grand Delegates that the officials of the Order were blinded by hate and could not see. They needed somebody with sight and balance to steady them.

I wanted to see if the National Body was as cancerous as the State Body. I went to Washington and found the infection in the National organization as I had found it in the State organization. The dominance of the same persons and the exercise of the same methods.

The dominant group was willing to take $2,500 and $1,700 from the Mortuary Fund but was not willing to pay the necessary administrative expenses to employees of the M. F. and of the Grand Council. The Acting Secretary Panetta, had worked for months and had demanded payment for his services, which was refused over and over again. Finally, when the question of loans was being discussed, the same Stephen Miele came to the Commission, as he had already gone to the Grand Council, to ask for a few hundred dollars for the payment of the services of the acting secretary, which were granted. This was at the meeting of December 14, 1925. He had come to the M. F. after having been pressed to pay personally, and through his brothers as he could no longer escape doom—the high discontent of Panetta and his possible leaving—which, by the way, would never have occured because of Panetta's hate for the other side.

The employees of the Order were overworked and under-paid. When I made attempts to pay them properly, the officers of the M. F. and of the Grand Council, said they had no money, in spite of the fact that there was enough money in the M. F. properly to pay its employees.

In August, 1926, when the offices of the M. F. and the Grand Council were obtained at 27 Cleveland Place, I was not even consulted concerning the employees of the commission who were nominated by Miele.

At the first meeting of the Mortuary Commission, the Commissioners began the proceedings in my absence, although I reached the meeting at 8:15.

I sat back and observed how far these people would go and at the end of the meeting I stood up for three-quarters of an hour and gave them a lesson they never forgot. I lectured them like a lot of school boys, and let them understand that I was not a decorative figure, but a real President of the Commission.

Open and free discussion was impossible. Every argument was considered a personal offense to the prominent people and to those who monopolize the Order and are, by the indifference of the masses, unused to being contradicted.

The predominating hypocrisy of the most influential and active of the leaders nauseated me. One of the most telling examples is furnished by Stephen Miele. At the crisis-meeting of January 12, 1926, of the M. F. Commission, he and his brother had acted like street rowdies, ruffians and blackguards. They thought that the secrecy of the meeting gave them full warrant to reek verbal abuse and physical assault upon an individual when no eyes were looking. Yet this man, capable of doing such acts, had the effrontery to stand up before the Washington Convention and tell that Washington Convention, (when he wanted money for the case against the Sons of Italy Grand Lodge, and was trying to arouse pity and their sympathy for the poor maltreated Schenectady side of the Order and for the Grand Venerable of that side), tell the whole history in detailed fashion of the encounter which nearly resulted in the physical clash of a Grand Venerable of the Sons of Italy Grand Lodge and Grand Venerable Freschi of the Schenectady group, at Conti's restaurant in the summer of 1925. This fiend without human feeling and human shame, who had done worse himself in company with his brother, at the meeting of January 12th of the Mortuary Commission, told the Delegates what a monstrous fiend was the person who was Grand Venerable of the Order Sons of Italy in the summer of 1925, for having gotten into an altercation with the Grand Venerable of the Schenectady group.

There was a brutality of words and of act which revolted.

At the beginning items were put upon the order of business by the Secretary of the Commission without consultation with me. So it happened that item 8 of the order of business of the meeting of October 29th, which appeared in a letter of October 26th, announcing the date of the meeting, was a proposal for the election of Stephen Miele to the position of Honorary Member of the M. F. Previous to the meeting on the meeting night, I took the secretary aside and asked him what it meant and why he had not consulted me. He said it was a "small matter and that it would be all right." The reader can imagine the condition I was in. I was trying to keep peace and harmony and at the same time, trying to protect my name for the future. I knew that a clash would come between the all-doer of the Order and me some time and that it might be said that I had been too easy in giving my aid in his becoming Honorary member of the Commission.

My dilemma was obvious; but the desire for peace and harmony prevailed. So I let it pass. At the meeting the proposal for the election of Miele to the position of Honorary Member was made by the Secretary and seconded by one of the members of the commission.

When the minutes of this meeting were written up and presented to me at my request, a few days before the November meeting, I remonstrated with the secretary because the minutes indicated that I was the proposer of the election of Miele to Honorary Membership.

On the meeting night in November, after the minutes had been read and I had explained to the Commissioners that I did not like the putting into the minutes of facts, which did not take place and indicated to the Commission one of them particularly, namely the one concerning the election of Miele, which the minutes set down as a proposal upon my part to the commission, I said to the Commission I should like to have the minutes changed to conform to the facts. The Secretary and the other members of the Commission urged me to accept the minutes as they were, pointing out to me that only an insignificant matter was involved. To me the matter was not insignificant. It was symptomatic and typical.

I decided after that evening, not to allow that sort of proceeding any longer, cost what it might in peace and harmony. And so it was that I wrote a letter to the Secretary, that from that time on the minutes should show the real proposer of any motion and not a fictitious proposer.

Mr. Mario De Pasquale: Dec. 18, 1925.

Secretary of F. U. M., 27 Cleveland Place, New York City.

Dear De Pasquale:

May I suggest to you a few ideas which arise out of the last meeting of the Commission on Monday night.

In making up the minutes, please let the minutes show the exact happenings at the Commission meeting. If you propose and expound any matter, kindly let the minutes show that. I do not desire credit that does not belong to me; nor do I desire to assume the responsibility after the event when I had nothing to do with the event itself.

Will you be good enough also to submit all circulars to me for approval before releasing them.

I should also be very glad if you would not forget to call my attention before every meeting of the Commission to important communications received and to be acted upon by the Commission apart from the order of business, which is communicated to every member of the Commission.

Will you also be good enough to put in the order of business for the next meeting the item to be taken up as to payment of bills for work which the Commission has not authorized. It seems to me that we ought to order something done or authorize it to be done before we are called upon to pay for expenditures already incurred.

RF/RJ   Cordially and fraternally yours,

CHAPTER V.

THE LUXURIANCE OF SUMMER
My Expenses for the Order
The Statement of Expenses

However base and low the actions of my opponents, it gives me an opportunity of presenting to the world not only what I have done for the Order but what I have actually expended out of my own pocket. I give here a statement of those expenses. The whole statement is not itemized but the itemized bills are in my possession.

Actual Expenses and Disbursements of Robert Ferrari during his connection with the Order Sons of Italy in America.

1.	Schenectady Convention—August, 1925	$ 50.00
2.	Washington Convention Jan. 31 to Feb. 2, 1926	60.00
3.	Articles: Nuovo Vessillo	72.50
	This includes review of Aquilano's book in 6 instalments on the History of The Sons of Italy.	
4.	Dictation and typewriting of Article Sons of Italy, A History	20.45
5.	Office Stenographer $10 a week for 24 weeks	240.00
6.	Special Stenographer Sons of Italy case	154.00
7.	Trip to Oyster Bay with Panetta, Sept. 1, 1925, taxi-fares and railroad fare	12.00

$608.95

Expenses Itemized

Public Stenographer   Tel.: Hanover 3586
 Notary Public

ALICE G. WALSKI
Singer Building
149 Broadway
Room 802

New York, November 10, 1925.

TO: Robert Ferrari, Esq.,
  165 Broadway, N. Y.

STATEMENT.

Re: Sons of Italy Case:

August	12	Memorandum in Re: Opinion		$28.50
	31	"	draft	20.40
Sept.	1	"	various	14.85
	8	"	of fact and law	38.50
Oct.	6	Brief		43.00
	6	Various papers		8.75

$154.00

Received Pay't. Nov. 12, 1925,
ALICE G. WALSKI

To Capparelli: For subscription to Nuovo Vessillo.

"		Aug. 14, 1925		$2.50
"	Articles	Oct. 14, 1925		15.00
"	"	Nov. 12, 1925		25.00
"	"	Dec. 15, 1925		15.00
"	"	Jan. 11, 1926		15.00

$72.50

Public Stenographer　　　　　　　　　　　Tel: Hanover 3586
Notary Public

ALICE G. WALSKI
Singer Building
149 Broadway
Room 802

New York, Nov. 10, 1925.

TO: Robert Ferrari, Esq.,
　　　　　　165 Broadway, New York.
Review of Book—B. Aquilano.
　Oct. 21
　　　26
　　　27
　Nov. 5
　　　8
　　　9
　　　10

　30 pp. 5 copies $20.45

　Rec'd payment Nov. 12, 1925.

ALICE G. WALSKI

STATE OF NEW YORK, ⎱ ss.:
COUNTY OF NEW YORK. ⎰

ALICE G. WALSKI, being duly sworn deposes and says:
She is a public stenographer with office at 149 Broadway,
Borough of Manhattan, City of New York.

That she acted as special stenographer to Robert Ferrari,
Esq., counselor at law, with offices at 165 Broadway, Borough
of Manhattan, City of New York, from August 9th to November
10, 1925.

That during this time she did stenographic and typewriting
work for the said Robert Ferrari, for which Robert Ferrari
paid her the sum of One Hundred seventy-four dollars and
forty-five cents ($174.45), itemized as follows:

Re: Sons of Italy Case.

August 12	Memorandum in Re: Opinion		$28.50
31	" draft		20.40
Sept. 1	" various		14.85
8	" of fact and law		38.50
Oct. 6	Brief		43.00
6	Various papers		8.75

$154.00

Oct. 21-6-7 and Nov. 5-8-9-10
      Review of B. Aquilano Book   20.45

Total... $174.45

ALICE G. WALSKI.

Sworn to before me this 12th day of May, 1926.

GEORGE E. BROWN.
Notary Public, Richmond County.

Certificate filed in N. Y. County No. 522

New York Register No. 7467

Term expires March 30, 1927

[Seal]

Not one cent of these expenses has ever been paid.

CHAPTER VI.

FOUL

Hitting Below the Belt—As Usual

The Loan:

Brabantio. Thou art a villain
Iago. You are—a senator.—Shakespeare.

Know, sense, like charity, begins at home.—Pope.

The trail of the serpent is over them all.—T. Moore.

No scandal about Queen Elizabeth, I hope.—R. B. Sheridan.

A very ancient and fish-like smell.—Shakespeare.

Remuneration! Oh, that's the Latin word for three farthings.
Remuneration! Why, it is a fairer name than French crown.—
Shakespeare.

> "Rancor to the right of them,
> Rancor to the left of them,
> Rancor in front of them,
> Rancor behind them,
> Volleyed and thundered.—Adapted from Tennyson.

All rising to great place is by a winding stair.—Bacon.

> In their faces stern defiance,
> In their hearts the feuds of ages,
> The hereditary hatred,
> The ancestral thirst of vengeance.—Longfellow.

A weak invention of the enemy.—Colley Cibber.
What should they know of England who only England know.—
Kipling.

Slander, meanest spawn of hell.—Tennyson.

CHAPTER VI.

FOUL

Hitting Below the Belt—As Usual

THE GUERDON OF LABOR

The Loan

But men like Miele do not understand any other motive, except the motive of money. They cannot conceive that a person may act with other motives. All the motives I have expounded, are motives enough if any were needed for me to take a lasting place of opposition to him and against all for which he stands.

In order to produce abiding hate what more can be done than what Miele has done to me. He has tried to drag me down to his own level and the level of the official atmosphere of the Order. He has tried in every way to contaminate me as well as everybody else who comes in contact with him and with the surroundings he moves in. He has used verbal threats against me, and his Brother Pasquale, acting at the instigation of Stephen, has attempted to use physical force upon me. If any cue to action were needed, have not I enough. And yet, for two months I remained silent and said I was done with the official part of the Order; that I didn't want to hear angthing about it; that it was impossible to live in the atmosphere of hate, of immorality and illegality which permeated every nook and corner of the officialdom of the Order; that the best thing a person could do to save his health, his reputation and his life, would be to stay a million miles away from it. The only credit I ever claimed for all the work I did there is the credit of having left the Order at the critical moment and before the Order had left any mark of its depravity upon me.

Oh, no, these motives are not enough for Miele. He has to begin first, an underground, whispering campaign, and then he has to have Caparelli, the Editor of the Nuovo Vessillo, in its issue of April 24, 1926, publish a summary of a speech Miele had delivered and to make prefatory remarks about that speech.

Capparelli is the man who came to my office at the head of a delegation of fifteen Grand Delegates to ask me to withdraw my resignation. He thought the Order would be dissolved into thin air if I left. He thought I should continue to lead that noble, band. He continually called me leader and so did all the rest and he and they said it was my business to remain in order to make my opinion and my position prevail against that of such scoundrels and blackguards as Miele. He said and they all said, that Miele was simply running true to form; what he had done to me is what he had done to other persons in the Order and to the Order itself, during the whole time of his connection with it. Caparelli cried. He wept and wept and wept. It was impossible to restrain the deluge of tears. He said if I stayed out of the Order the end of the world would come. I do not blame poor Capparelli much. I understand.

This is what The Nuovo Vessillo published on page 3, quoting from a speech made by Stephen Miele at the initiation of a Lodge.

> "The truth is that Robert Ferrari needed money and began by having some one ask me for $500 just as he had asked $1,000 of another friend and brother. As he did at other times he turned to Brother Panetta and Panetta turned to my Brother Humbert, who declared himself ready to endorse a note signed by Counsellor Ferrari, but Ferrari urgently demanded the money without much ceremony. This is the true reason of his attitude and of his decision."

So I did not want the endorsements of a promissory note; I wanted money immediately and in cash.

I had already asked another person for $1,000.

I had Panetta go to Miele's brother Humbert to get the money. I needed the money urgently, and I wanted it without too many compliments.

Even if this story were true, the baseness of the individual who could tell it is sufficiently manifested by the story itself, and the editor of the newspaper who comes to my office and begs me upon his knees, in the presence of 15 delegates and cries practically uninterruptedly, during a long session, for my return to the Order, a man who had a thousand times expounded my good qualities to others, and in a 20-minute speech before the Delegates, praised me to the skies, this man takes the words of this hyena in human form, and not only publishes them in his paper, but actually comments upon them and sustains the hyena's position.

Capparelli says "Robert Ferrari, not knowing, not being able or not willing to fight as a man of courage, of faith and of honor, retired in heroic—comical fashion from the arena of combat * * * thus repudiating not only his friends but also the institution of which he desired to appear to be the new apostle or the new Messiah. We give on this page the most relevant points of the speech of Chev. Miele, which was listened to with the greatest interest."

Et sic transit gloria mundi.

See what they said of me once:

Nuovo Vessillo of December 12, 1925.

Extracts from an article called "The Monographs of Counsellor Ferrari."

> "He (Robert Ferrari), has devoted himself with loving intellect and with a spirit of generous sacrifice to the triumph

of our cause and has put at the service of our Grand Lodge, his powerful intelligence, his profound legal culture and his phenomenal activity" * * *

In the Vessillo of October 10, 1925:

"We expounded the precious and effective collaboration which Counsellor Ferrari has given, in respect to legal matters to our Grand Council, especially in the drawing up of the historical and colossal memorial of 180 printed pages presented to the Supreme Court of Utica to obtain the injunction against the Sons of Italy Grand Lodge."

"In the issue of November 7th we published the preface to the magnificent brief which is a patient and exhaustive analysis of the schism in the Grand Lodge of the State of New York, of which he treats with argumentative force the legal and the moral side of the question."

(Extract from Nuovo Vessilo, October 17, 1925.)

Initiation of "Nicola Misari" Lodge at the Sons of Italy Hall East 15th St.

"Speaking of speeches we are sorry not to have been able to take down in shorthand the speech—rich in sane concepts and in serene and constructive criticism, made by the illustrious jurist, Robert Ferrari, President of the F. U M. It was more than a speech; it was a picture in which Counselor Ferrari showed himself to be also a learned sociologist and a profound student of the problems of immigration in relation to the associative life of our colonies, in respect to the progress of the Order and in regard to the future of the Italian Community in America."

The truth of the matter can be said in a very few words. I could deny it and play the trick they play, of denying what there is of the truth. In my case I should be highly justified, if ever the end justified the means. They have given us a torrent of general and specific denials; and even persons who were never present at conversations or events, have denied the existence of the facts. If I had not the documents these people would all get together and try to prove almost anything they could frame up against me.

Fortunately for me they have nothing on me. They enter a general denial of the accusations I bring against them. They make statements without proof and without the possibility of proof. They have no documents and they rely on the solidarity of the gang to pull them through. I do not make any statements which I cannot prove, and I can prove the charges I make, not by the testimony of interested and depraved witnesses but by the testimony of unimpeachable documents written long before there was any reason for falsification.

I had been working, as is indicated in another portion of this pamphlet, for about three months, August, September and October, almost every minute of the day and night for our case against the Sons of Italy Grand Lodge. This required not only an enormous expenditure of labor, an expenditure of labor that Capparelli in his paper elaborated very fully upon, but an enormous expenditure of energy and of money. I must have lost several thousands of dollars during these three months when I could not do my own business. My office was completely given over to the Sons of Italy. I could not take in any new cases and I could not even properly attend to some of my old cases.

The work required in the Sons of Italy case was not only long, involved and elaborate, but had to be done under the greatest pressure. What I did for the Order as counsel would, if I had put in a bill, have cost the Order a professional fee of $10,000.

My expenses run up to hundreds of dollars a week and for eleven or twelve weeks there was a constant expenditure from my little store. I was expecting to receive several large fees. I had a great many credits outstanding from clients, who owed me for professional services rendered. Those who know me, know I do not desire to press; and even if I had wanted to press I should not have had the time to do it then. My financial condition very soon would be capable of bearing me on for weeks without a fee from the plaintiffs in the Sons of Italy case.

When the Grand Venerable said I was entitled to a retainer in the beginning of the case in August, I offered to accept it, but surely I am not to be blamed for this. The American lawyers had received a similar retainer, and all lawyers demand, and rightly demand, retainers. But no retainer was forthcoming. I never obtained a cent from them, in spite of actual disbursements suffered by me, stenographer's fees and expenses of travelling.

In the month of November the American law firm insisted upon its retainer of $25,000 or it would have to abandon the case. The firm desired to know how much the lawyers, who were members of the Order Sons of Italy wished as their share, the retainer and the whole fee being dependent upon the value of our services to the Order and the American firm desiring to set its fee according to the exigencies and the demands of all the attorneys and counsel in the case.

A meeting of those lawyers, who were members of the law Committee of the Order was called in the office of the Grand Venerable Freschi, where the question of our fees was discussed and decided. Miele wanted his fee—for what I do not know. He probably was asking for a fee for his services in going down to the attorneys' offices and giving them the so-called facts of the case. Being a veteran of the Order and being mixed up in all the practices of the Order for many years, he knew the ins and outs of the happenings. His attitude would have made anybody boil. The Grand Venerable asked me how much I asked as my fee and I told him I could give him my decision immediately; I desired no fee at all. This was in December, when my financial condition had bettered and I was able not only to say to the Grand Venerable, in the presence of two other members of the Committee, that I declined to accept a fee for all the services I had rendered and would render, but that I would also contribute to the cause the actual disbursements out of my own pocket, which I had made up to that time and which amounted to several hundreds of dollars, and those which I would in the future make. The Grand Venerable said, "I thought you would say that."

Unfortunately, the latter part of October, as I have said, I desired a little financial help to tide me over for about 30 days. Panetta and I had been mutually helpful and since he, as he has said on many occasions, and as he said before the committee of 15 Grand Delegates, at my office, was deeply indebted to me in the realms of the intellect and the spirit and since he was engrossed in the winning of the case we talked the matter over. He was giving his services for nothing too. We had worked together on phases of the case up to 3 o'clock in the morning. He undertook, as a friendly office, to procure for me, upon my promissory note payable in 30 days, a loan of $500.00. To whom he went and where, I did not know. I found out two weeks afterwards that he had been to Humbert Miele and that the latter had declined to lend any money either by the actual giving of cash or by the putting of his endorsement upon a promissory note. Panetta went so far as to ask him for a personal loan—Panetta, who knew a victory for the Order was a victory for the clan. Panetta afterwards told me this and he could have testified — could have testified before he sold himself body and soul and before he descended to the lowest depths a human being can drop to as we shall presently see—to the horror with which I took the news. Now he will testify to anything to hang me. I told him that it was a red letter day in the annals of my life when they refused, knowing them as I did; if they had given it and I had accepted they would have considered me in their power for ever after; if they had not given it, they would bring that up in the future as the motive for any attitude of mine toward them. Oh, my prophetic soul!

The relations between Miele and myself during my whole connection with the Order Sons of Italy were of the most distant kind. From the beginning we were mutually hostile and repulsive to each other. We both felt that we did not belong to the same category of human being.

During the whole nine months that I was connected with the Order, no man ever saw us shake hands; nor did any shaking of hands ever take place when nobody was looking!

He put pressure upon the Secretary of the Commission and made that poor man, who was dependent upon the Order, an instrument of his will. It was due to him that the minutes were inaccurate. It was to benefit him that the minutes were falsified. It was he, himself, who put the screws upon the helpless secretary of the Commission to make him do his will.

Wherever he went in the Order, he had to be the main gazabo. No other, not even the Grand Venerable, in spite of the fact that he was using the Grand Venerable for his purpose, could shine while he was present. Whether at the Grand Convention or at the Supreme Convention, it was he who had to be refulgent. During and after the Washington Convention, I heard it said that it was stupid and egotistic upon his part and upon the part of the Grand Venerable to take and keep the centre of the stage themselves and throw into the shadow the Grand Orator of the Order.

He and the gang wanted to drag the Order into all the squabbles and quarrels, the ruptures and the schisms. Whereever there was a fight and the other side was in it, Miele and the gang wanted us to go into it. For example: There was an alarm sent out in December, 1925, because it was said the New York Convention group were trying to bring about a coup d'etat in the Italian Hospital administration. Therefore, the Schenectady group had to put on its war feathers and go out en masse with its most destructive batteries, to the meeting of the Italian Hospital and annihilate the opposition. It was necessary to have representatives at that meeting and inasmuch as the M. F. had been represented by two Delegates, Miele came to the M. F. commission meeting and asked for $200 so that we might have representation in the Italian Hospital Executive Committee to fight his personal battles with.

To sum up the whole situation—the methods of this Stephen Miele are the methods of oppression, of force, of the camorra and of the mafia.

Circular No. 2 has the effrontery to call me a metaphysician, and to call the officials of the Order practical men. Yet, it is the metaphysician and the metaphysician alone, who has shown not only adherence to principles but actually has descended to the highly practical detail work of the highly practical man and gotten a series of documents to prove my case, which as a metaphycian I should not have been able to gather together.

I had asked $1000 of another friend and brother. This is even more simple. Out of the generosity of my nature and the desire to make others happy in sharing my happiness, I had, in the middle of November, lent $1,000 to Panetta who was starving and who was knocking at the doors of the F. U. M. and the Grand Council for pay for his services.

This man had shown that check, as I long afterwards found out by accident—from Panetta himself—to Stephen Miele and others. When I said: why did you show it? he answered—"I wanted to show how solid you were, and the character of man you are." Panetta at that time and for two years had boosted me everywhere and always as a superman. Oh! these cracked creatures who today praise to the skies and tomorrow, for no rhyme or reason, will run you into the ground! Miele, with his wild imaginings, with his highly "practical" nature and with a disposition which makes it impossible for him even to begin to roam upon the outskirts of the decent instincts of humanity, immediately inferred that I had borrowed $1,000 and was now paying it back.

How anybody can lend $1,000 to anybody else is inconceivable to one as avaricious and ignoble as Miele. Such magnanamity and nobility of spirit is far beyond his wildest imaginings.

If Miele desires, I shall be glad to present him with a real, true and genuine photographic copy—not doctored like his minutes—of the check. On second thought: Here it is! (See Appendix 5).

Panetta has fallen so low—another victim of the Order—as to tell people that he and his brother lent me money. Like the Ancient Mariner in Coleridge's poem he stoppeth one of three. Indeed, he goes farther; he stops everybody he meets and then tells people that he and his brother lent me money.

What relevancy this has to the issues in the Order Sons of Italy case I do not know, nor can anybody else see except persons of the depraved and irrational mind of Panetta and of Miele. It is true that he lent me a few hundred dollars before August, 1925; and that his brother also lent me two hundred dollars after August, 1925. But it is also true that I paid back the loans. The argument they use is a non-sequitur. The conclusion does not follow from the premises. They say that my motive in attacking Miele at the present time and the rest of the gang is, that I could not get a loan from Miele. The Argument ought to work the other way also. If I did get a loan from somebody I should not now attack them. Now, I admit that I did get a loan from Panetta; yet at the present time, since he has lied about me and related private things, which no gentleman would relate, I am attacking him as I am attacking the others.

In fact he has proven himself to be the lowest and worst, because my relations with him were closest and his indebtedness to me was greatest.

Panetta is subdued to what he works in. He looks on at a change made in the minutes of the F. U. M. Commission and stands by the purity of the minutes without a wink. This in the presence of a reporter of a daily paper. He is the man who is now writing the metaphysical circulars against me, like the letter to the Press of April 16, 1926 and the circulars, like circular No. 21 of April 19th.

Every school boy remembers the passage in Macaulay's essay on Milton.

I advise members of the Grand Council, Miele and Panetta, to read it. The first part runs something like this. I quote from memory:

"We charge him with having violated his coronation vows."

And they reply:

"He was a good father and a kind husband."

I charge them with high crimes and misdemeanors.

And they retort:

"You have a black tie."

Their argument is insignificant, irrelevant and extraneous. They do not use the argument used by the defenders of Charles I, as in the Macaulay passage. This would be not only understandable but at least, reveal to the world some of the good qualities which they have—if they have any. But they do not contend in their argument that they have any good qualities at all. They just use an argument which has nothing to do with the matter. Again, they do not even use a tuquoque argument. They do not say: You are just as bad as we are. If we have committed illegal and immoral acts, you too have committed illegal and immoral acts. We might go down the whole list of logical and rhetorical arguments that may be used in a debate and find these paragons of virtue and of intellgence, do not use any of them, but dive down into the mud and pick up a private matter, which even if true, would, like the flowers that bloom in the Spring in the Gilbert & Sullivan opera, have nothing to do with the case.

Their reasoning is magnificent—but it is not war. The clan and Panetta were Members of a Club I was a member of and I delivered a phillippic against the administration of the Club. This phillippic happened to coincide with the wishes of the clan and Panetta. This might indicate to an impartial world, that in spite of my rancor, if I had any thing against the clan, I took a line which I believed to be right, notwithstanding the fact that my labors benefited them. People at the time, In December, 1925, who did not know the inside workings of the machine, might have thought—and did think—that I was hand in glove with the clan and that I was doing their work. The fact of the matter is, that their desires happened to coincide with my course of action and they took advantage of my criticism of the administration of the club. But if the reasoning, which they now employ, is sound I should not have spoken in favor of the position they held, because I had a grudge against them. The reasoning of this group leads, therefore, to extraordinary conclusions.

Panetta had nothing to do with my going up to Schenectady or with convincing me that the case of Sons of Italy Grand Lodge was right. I made an independent study of the documents and the situation of the case and I was finally turned to the position of opponent of the Sons of Italy Grand Lodge at the very last moment, particularly because of certain methods used by the Sons of Italy Grand Lodge and certain documents including telegrams, which I knew, as a lawyer, coul dnot be true.

These $200 which Panetta had lent me he had lent months before August, 1925, under the following circumstances:

He had recommended to me a client in a criminal libel case. The work I did was worth $1,000 at least and I was willing because of the recommendation and other facts, to charge only $600. The client said he was not able to pay that sum of money and paid only about $100 and no more. I told Panetta how much time I had spent upon it and the character of work that had to be done and he made up the deficiency of his friend by turning over to me $200 in this way as a loan partly making up for the difficulties his friend had put me into.

Does Panetta also say to the reader or to any one in private conversation, that when he came to me two or three days after the combined meeting of January 15th, when a resolution was passed making a recommendation to the M. F. to make a loan of $2,500 to the Grand Council for the payment of attorneys' fees, he was a raving maniac. The reason for his lunacy was the fact that everybody had jumped upon him because he had not produced accurate minutes of the Grand Council and M. F. Commission meeting of January 15, 1926.

On the 22nd day of January, a meeting of the Mortuary Commission was held at which the Commission was to act upon the recommendation made by the Grand Council at the combined meeting of January 15th, for the granting of the loan of $2,500 on that date. Before the beginning of the meeting I asked Panetta for a copy of the minutes of that meeting. Panetta gave me the minutes. I read them over and I found no recommendation by the Grand Council concerning the $2,500 loan. I therefore felt justified in not proceeding that evening with a vote upon the loan.

That was the night I had a long conversation after the meeting with Freschi at the Hotel Astor, in which I told him that no vote on the loan had taken place and why. Everybody was furious at Panetta. All those at the combined meeting insisted upon the fact that the resolution recommending the loan had been made. Panetta, on the contrary, had suppressed that resolution and substituted another resoluton recommendng to the Commission to divide the funds of the Commission into two parts, one of $1 from each member and one of the monthly contributions.

Panetta passed a long, bad quarter of an hour. His castle, built upon hate, was rapidly crumbling. Since the real matter had to come to a vote I thought I would save him from mutilation by the members of the Order by calling a special meeting of the M. F. in order to decide the question which had been recommended for favorable decision by the Grand Council at the combined meeting of January 15th—a recommendation which had not appeared in the minutes as drawn up by Panetta. I could, since I had a sufficient excuse for not calling another meeting on account of the shortness of time, have sent the Grand Delegates to Washington without a vote. But I took pity upon him. He was an old war horse of the Order, his whole life was wrapped up in the fight and I knew that he would be forever damned and ruined if the mistake he had made in the minutes had not been rectified by the calling of another meeting of the M. F. to vote upon the question of a loan. All this he knows.

This is the man who now wallows in the most base-born conduct. He talks about a loan to me to whomever he meets. Fortunate me! that this is all they can say against me! Morgan, too, obtains loans.

The Order Sons of Italy is a public institution; and all those connected with it ought to lead a public life. No secrets should be hidden. I have exposed all my secret doings to the world.

I challenge Miele and the gang to expose their shady practices.

The Order must be dragged into all fights. The Order could not be let alone but whenever there was some activity on the part of the opposition, even outside the Order, that activity had to be suppressed or counteracted by activity on the part of our group. The circle gradually grew so large that it almost included the universe. So it was with the Italian hospital.

Panetta came to see me one morning and brought an Italian paper, which announced a meeting of the administrative body of the Italian Hospital. He asked what I thought of it. I told him I did not see anything extraordinary about it. By this time Panetta had lost his temper so rapidly, that he had very litle left and so he became excited and said that the other side, the Sons of Italy group, were trying to dominate the Italian Hospital. The gang kept pounding on this subject for days until they came before the Commission to ask for $200 to get into the fight with. By the payment of $100 the Grand Council and the M. F. would have the right to a representative in the Committee of the Hospital.

CHAPTER VII.

CROSS-EXAMINATION

Questions to Freschi

1. Did Ferrari vote in favor of the granting of the loan or against?

2. Did you say in caucus of the New York Delegation in Washington before the whole Delegation, that you had the check for $2,500 and that the members of the Commsision had voted according to their lights?

3. Did you refer to me as the one who had voted against the granting of the loan?

4. Did Miele want a fee for his services as Counsel to the Grand Lodge?

5. When did Miele say that he did not want a fee for those services?

6. Did I at your office, in December, 1925, say that I did not want a fee for my services as counsel to the Grand Lodge?

7. Did I not also say at that time that I did not want to be paid for my disbursements?

8. Did you call that meeting of counsel in the case to decide what fee should go to each counsel?

9. Did you call it at the suggestion of the American firm who wanted to know how much counsel in the case desired in order properly to distribute their retainer?

10. Did you, when I declined to accept any fee, say these words—"that is just like you; I thought you would say that?"

11. Did Miele ask for a fee that day?

12. How much did he ask?

13. Did any other counsel in the case, among the Italians, ask for any fee except Miele?

14. Did I, on the night of January 15, 1926, immediately preceding the combined meeting of the Grand Council and Mortuary Commission, take you, Angrisani and Panetta aside and tell you what had happened at the meeting of January 12th, at which Miele and his brother Pasquale, had used abusive language to me and had attempted to strike me?

15. Did I tell you that Stephen Miele had said the following:

    1. "If we had not done illegal and immoral things in the Order, we would never have done anything in the past.

    2. You (referring to me) do not know law.

    3. If a Supreme Court Justice can do illegal and immoral things, you (referring to me) can.

    4. You (referring to me) think you are intelligent. You will see. I'll fix you."

16. Did I not indicate to you the manner in which he said these words, particularly the last, when he was going to fix me for my opposition to the loan?

17. Did I tell you then, in the presence of Angrisani and Panetta, that things could not go on that way and that Miele would have to eliminate himself or I would eliminate myself?

18. Did you say that Miele's actions were outrageous and that you would speak to him immediately, to eliminate him from the Commission?

19. Is it true that you did?

20. Did I also tell you what his brother Pasquale had said and done?

21. On the evening of January 22nd did I meet you at the Hotel Astor as I was coming into the Bar Association meeting and you were coming out, and did I not speak to you for over three hours in the lobby and give you in detail what had happened at the meeting of the Mortuary Commission that evening concerning the voting on the loan?

22. Did I tell you that no vote had been taken and why?

23. Did I tell you that no vote had been taken because the minutes of the combined meeting, written up by Panetta, did not authorize me to do so and that they authorized me to put to a vote only this question, whether the funds of the Order should be divided?

24. Did you say that you did not know what to do; that it was vital for us to have the loan?

25. Did I not tell you that the loan could be gotten in another way?

26. Had I not told you several times before how the money could be gotten?

27. Did you not insist that night, that the money should be gotten out of the M. F.?

28. Is it not a fact that when you went away that night, you thought it might not be possible to hold another meeting of the Mortuary Commission before the Washington Convention?

29. Did I write to you two or three days before the Washington Convention, telling you that I was eager to resign and did I give you some reasons.

Questions to Angrisani

(Member of Grand Council)

1. Did I, on the night of the combined meeting of the Grand Council and Mortuary Fund January 15, 1926, call you, the Grand Venerable and Panetta aside before the meeting, and did I for over an hour tell you the details of what had happened on the night of January 12th at the M. F. Commission meeting?

2. Did I tell you that Stephen Miele made the following statements:

1. "If we had not done illegal and immoral things in the Order, we would never have done anything in the past.

2. You (referring to me) do not know law.

3. If a Supreme Court Justice can do illegal and immoral things, you (referring to me) can.

4. You (referring to me) think you are intelligent. You will see."

3. Did I tell you that both Stephen Miele and his brother Pasquale used vile and foul language?

4. Did I tell you that both brothers used abusive terms to Ferrari?

5. Did I tell you that Pasquale Miele at that meeting attempted to strike Ferrari?

6. Did Ferrari also tell you various other means of obstruction that Stephen Miele used against Ferrari in his work as President of the Commission?

Questions to M. De Pasquale

1. Did I invite you to dinner on the night of January 12, 1926?

2. Did I at that dinner, previous to the meeting of the M. F. of that night, say to you that we had come to the crossing of the ways and that it was necessary for you to be either with me or against me?

3. Did I not tell you that I could no longer allow the pressure of Miele upon you and the Members of the Commission to influence the proceedings of the Commission?

4. Did I not ask you why you had kept out of the minutes the fact that Stephen Miele had proposed a loan of $2,500 at the meeting of December 14, 1925?

5. Did I ask you directly whether he had told you to do it?

6. Did you hesitate in answering?

7. Did you say "N-o--, but I know the type of man he is"?

8. Have you worked in the Order with Miele for the last 20 years?

9. Do you know his character?

10. Do you know that he wanted you, even if he had not told you, to falsify the minutes in his favor?

11. Is it not true, that he asked you directly, not to put into the minutes, the fact of his appearance before the Commission with the proposal of the loan?

12. Is it not true that I wrote you, even before the 14th of December, 1925, telling you that the minutes were inexact?

13. Did I not tell you that I desired no credit for proposals I did not make and that the minutes were to be an exact reflection of what happened at the meetings?

14. Did I not tell you that I desired no responsibility for what did not happen at the meetings and that if the minutes were exact, that responsibility would not be upon my shoulders?

15. Did I ever object to your sending out circulars to the

Subordinate Lodges and letters to the Press, without first having submitted them to me?

16. Did you ever do that, send out communications to the Press—and circulars to subordinate lodges without consulting with me?

17. Did I object to that proceeding?

18. Did I tell you that all circulars and communications to the press were to be first submitted to me?

19. Did Stephen Miele come to the Commission on December authorized by resolution of the Grand Council to propose a loan of $2,500?

20. Did he present this resolution?

21. If he did present this resolution, is the resolution spread out or mentioned in the minutes?

22. Can you show it?

Questions—Stephen Miele

1. Did you come before the Mortuary Commission on the 14th of December, 1925, to ask for a loan of $2,500 from the Commission to the Grand Council to pay attorneys' fees with?

2. Did you come of your own initiative?

3. Did you come after consultation with any officer of the Grand Council?

4. Were you authorized to come by resolution of the Grand Council?

5. Were you authorized to come by the suggestion of a member of the Grand Council?

6. If you come authorized by resolution, show the resolution in the Grand Council minutes?

7. Did you appear before the Mortuary Commission again on the matter of a loan of $2,500 on the 12th of January, 1926?

8. On the same evening did you come to ask for an additional loan of $1,700 to pay the expenses of the Grand Delegates?

9. At the meeting of January 12th of the Mortuary Commission were you authorized by the Grand Council to ask for either loans?

10. If you were authorized by the Grand Council, present the resolution of the Grand Council or show the resolution in the minutes?

11. Is it true that on the night of the meeting of the Mortuary Commission of January 12th, you made the following statements:

1. "If we had not done illegal and immoral things in the Order, we would never have done anything in the past.

2. You (referring to me) do not know law.

3. If a Supreme Court Justice can do illegal and immoral things, you (referring to me) can.

4. You (referring to me) think you are intelligent. You will see?"

12. Did you want a fee for your work as counsel to the Grand

Lodge in the case of the Order Sons of Italy vs. the Sons of Italy Grand Lodge?

13. How much did you ask?

14. Did any other counsel ask for a fee?

15. Were you the only one to ask for a fee?

16. Did you ignore representatives of mine whom I sent to take my place at meetings of subordinate lodges?

17. Did you suppress parts of my letters sent to the Subordinate Lodges when you assumed the authority to read the letters at those meetings?

18. Did you say to me in August, 1925, coming up Broadway from the offices of the American firm, in the presence of Panetta, after retainers had been talked about in the American firm's office and no retainers were forthcoming, that I need not worry and that I could get rich upon the Order?

19. Did your brother, on the night of the meeting of the M. F. of January 12th, call me vile names?

20. Did he also come up close to me and raise his arm in an attempt to strike me?

21. Did you tell De Pasquale not to put in the minutes the fact that you appeared at the meeting of December 14th of the M. F. to ask for a loan of $2,500.00?

22. Did you tell De Pasquale not to put into the minutes, the fact that you had appeared before the Commission on January 12, 1926, to ask for a loan of $2,500 and for lawyers' fees and $1,700 for Grand Delegates to the Washington Convention?

23. Did you at a meeting of lawyers and laymen in the office of the American lawyers, turn to Robert Ferrari and in the presence of the members of the Committee present say—"Ferrari will cross-examine Cotillo?"

24. Did not Ferrari answer immediately: "Ferrari will not cross-examine Cotillo."

Questions to the Members of the Mortunary Fund

1. On the 14th of December, 1925, and the 12th of January, 1926, at the meetings of the Mortuary Commission, when Stephen Miele appeared to propose the loan of $2,500 and the loan of $1,700 at the meeting of January 12th, 1926, did he come authorized by resolution of the Grand Council?

2. If he did, did he present that resolution?

3. If he did present the resolution, is the resolution spread out or mentioned in the minutes?

4. At the meeting of January 12, 1926, did Stephen Miele make the following statements?

    1. "If we had not done illegal and immoral things in the Order, we would never have done anything in the past.

    2. You (referring to me) do not know law.

    3. If a Supreme Court Justice can do illegal and immoral things, you (referring to me) can.

4. You (referring to me) think you are intelligent. You will see. I'll fix you."

5. Did Pasquale Miele at that meeting, use abusive terms to Ferrari and did he attempt to strike him?

Questions to Ali Prandi
(Member of the F. U. M.)

1. Did Miele on the night of December 14, 1925, at which he proposed a loan of $2,500, come authorized by resolution?

2. Was I opposed to the proposal; at the meeting of January 12th did Miele again appear before the Commission to ask for a loan of $2,500 and $1,700?

3. Was I opposed to the loan?

4. Did I at the meeting of December 14th and January 12th, give at length my reasons for my objecting?

5. At the meeting of January 12, 1926, did Miele come authorized by the Grand Council to make the proposal?

6. Did he at this meeting of January 12th, make the following statements:

    1. "If we had not done illegal and immoral things in the Order, we would never have done anything in the past.

    2. You (referring to me) do not know law.

    3. If a Supreme Court Justice can do illegal and immoral things, you (referring to me) can.

    4. You (referring to me) think you are intelligent. You will see."

Note for the Reader:

Ali Prandi called me up on May 3rd and told me he had taken no part in the meeting which decided upon the communication to the Press, which appeared in the Corriere April 26, 1926. He also stated he has been disgusted ever since the meeting of January 12th, when they treated Ferrari so badly.

He is one of the leaders in the peace movement to bring together both sides. They already have had several meetings. He regretted that this quarrel had begun and desired to see harmony reign.

He was unaware of the communications to the Press. I told him to read them first, before he talked of peace between the Miele gang and me.

7. Did Pasquale Miele at that meeting, use abusive terms to Ferrari and did he attempt to strike him?

Questions—Frank Panetta

1. Isn't it true that you hate Cotillo so much, that you would do anything and say anything, no matter how ruinous to the reputation of anybody, to keep together your group of the Order Sons of Italy, in order with that group to destroy Cotillo, whom you so hate?

2. Before the Conventions at New York and at Schenectady,

did you urge me to go to meetings at the Hotel Pennsylvania of the Miele-Freschi group, who were planning a course of action?

3.   Is it or is it not true, that you came of your own initiative?

4.   If you did not come of your own initiative, who sent you?

5.   Is it true or is it not true, that at the end of July, you called me on the 'phone and said that you had been delegated to ask me whether I would not come to the meeting of the Schenectady group at the Hotel Pennsylvania?

6.   Did I ever attend a meeting of that group at the Hotel Pennsylvania or elsewhere?

7.   Did you want me to act as Special Grand Orator to prosecute the Members of the Grand Council of the State of New York, who were then up on charges before the Supreme Arbitration Committee?

8.   Did I accept and did I act as Special Grand Orator?

9.   During one month previous to the Convention in August, 1925, did I spend any more than 5 or 6 hours with you?

(No. 9.   I was trying to avoid him because I did not desire to be connected with the mess.)

10.   Did Miele say, or did he not say, to me, coming up from the American lawyers' office one day in August, that I would make a lot of money in the Order?

11.   Did I reply?

12.   What did I tell you after he left us? That he was crazy?

13.   Was I not against a loan of $2,500 and of $1,700?

14.   Did not Miele, at both times, December 14th, 1925, and January 12th, 1926, come before the Commission without authorization from the Grand Council?

15.   Did I ever speak to you of the importance of the resolution of the question of the loans in the proper manner, and did I not say that the gang were trying to ruin me and were persistent in their efforts to do so?

16.   Did I not tell you that I wanted to get out of the mess as soon as possible?

17.   Did you not insist that the loan of $2,500 be given?

18.   Did I not oppose that position?

19.   Did you not get mad because I did not want to grant the loan?

20.   On the night of the 15th day of January, did I not call you, Freschi and Angrisani aside, previous to the beginning of the meeting of the combined Grand Council and Mortuary Fund Commission, and tell you in detail for over an hour, what had taken place at the meeting of the Commissioner, of January 12th, at which Miele and his brother abused me with words and attempted to attack me by physical force?

21.   Was I not against a loan on the night of January 15th at the meeting?

22.   Do not the minutes written up by you, of that meeting, show that I was against the loan?

23.   Do these minutes not show that another meeting of the

Mortunary Fund was to be held for the purpose of dividing the fund into two parts, one the part lent to the commission at the rate of $1 a piece from each member of the Lodges pertaining to the F. U. M. and the other, money received by the M. F. from monthly contributions?

24. Did not the M. F. hold a meeting on the 22nd day of January, 1926, as a result of the combined meeting of January 15, to act upon the resolution of that combined meeting, and did I not before the meeting, ask you for a copy of the minutes which you gave me, and did I not say to you, that the minutes did not indicate the fact that the M. F. was to vote on the loan of $2,500 but only that the M. F. was to vote that night upon the question of the division of the funds?

25. Did not Members of the Commission and others, say to you that the minutes were wrong; that the combined meeting had made a recommendation to the M. F. Commissioners to lend the money to the Grand Council?

26. Did I not afterwards tell you that I did not put the question of the loan to the Grand Council because the minutes which you had given me a copy of, did not authorize me to put the matter to a vote; and that the only thing that they authorized me to do was to put to vote the question of the division of the funds?

27. Did I not tell you afterwards, that I would not put the matter to a vote and that I should not be fully enough protected in my opposition to the loan, unless there was a recommendation from the Grand Council to have a vote upon the loan?

28. Did I not tell you that the same evening of January 22nd, I had gone to a meeting of the Bar Association at the Hotel Astor and had met Freschi, with whom I had talked 3 hours, giving him the result of the proceedings of the Mortuary Commission, at which no vote had been taken?

29. Did you not come down to my office between the 22nd and 29th days of January after having telephoned me several times telling me about the revolution in the Order and that I was considered a tyrant and an autocrat because I would not put the matter to a vote?

30. Did you not act like a raving mad man in my office because I did not put the matter to a vote without the proper authorization which I had requested from the Grand Council?

31. Did Stephen Miele come to the Commission on December 14th authorized by resolution of the Grand Council to propose a loan of $2,500?

32. Did he present this resolution? If he did present this resolution is the resolution spread out or mentioned in the minutes? Can you show it?

33. Did I say to you that I would put the matter to a vote if the authorization of the Grand Council were given and the authorization put on file with the Mortuary Commission?

34. Did you relate our interview to Freschi and was there

presented instead of a resolution of the Grand Council a letter, which stated that the Mortuary Commission could take that in lieu of a resolution? Was this letter signed by every member of the Grand Council except two?

35. Is it true that this letter was not presented to me until the night of the meeting of January 29th, 1926?

36. Is it true that I had asked for a resolution and that this letter was given instead?

37. Is it true that since my resignation, I have seen you only two times, once at a private gathering and once at the meeting of the Grand Delegates at my offiec?

38. Isn't it true that you told me that everybody was blaming you because you had written up the minutes of the combined meeting of January 15th and that although the minutes should have shown what it was contended was the truth, namely, that the meeting had resolved to make a recommendation to the Mortuary Commission to grant the loan and to bring the matter to a vote, you had omitted that and had substituted a resolution recommending to the M. F. Commission to divide the M. F. into two parts, one part, the loans made at $1 a piece to the Commission and the second, the sums gathered by monthly contributions?

39. In August, September and October did you have many quarrels with the employees in the office and did you threaten to leave?

40. Did you want things which the Miele clan would not give you and in spite of this did you remain?

41. Did I not tell you that the clan did not take seriously your threats to leave because they knew that you would not leave?

42. Did I not tell you that the reason they would not give you a cent of salary or give you any facilities in the office was because they knew, that under any circumstances, you would stay, because your hatred for judge Cotillo was so great that you would suffer anything rather than lose the opportunity of mauling and destroying judge Cotillo?

43. At the Grand Delegates' meeting at the office of Robert Ferrari in February, 1926, when Capparrelli said that Lodges would leave the Schenectady group if and when they found out about the resignation of Robert Ferrari, did you say that he was crazy and that no lodge would leave on account of the resignation of Ferrari?

44. It is true that now that a revolution has broken out in your group by the resignation of Ferrari and your words have proved to be unprophetic, you are willing because of your hate for judge Cotillo and your desire to win at all costs, to malign Ferrari and try to blacken his reputation, even going to the extent of lying about private matters that have nothing to do with the affairs of the Order?

F. Panetta

Private Questions

4.   Is it the part of a gentleman, even if you have lent some one money, to say to a third party that you have lent the money?

5.   Isn't it true that Ferrari did not know that you were going to Miele to ask him for money for Ferrari?

6.   Isn't it true that you asked Humbert Miele for a personal loan to you and that he refused?

7.   Isn't it true that you were very angry because of the fact that he did not appreciate your work in the Order and what you had done to save the skin of the Miele clan, and that you said he was an ingrate not to lend you $200 when he had nearly over a quarter of a million dollars?

8.   Isn't it true that you have called all the Mieles "bad eggs and rotters"?

9.   Isn't it true that you went to your brother to ask him for a loan without my knowledge, as you had done in the case of Humbert Miele?

10.   Isn't it true that you did get $200 from your brother, that you brought your brother to my office and that it was then I knew where you had gotten the loan to me from?

11.   Isn't it true that I owed you $195 on the 12th of November, 1925?

12.   Isn't it true that on the 12th of November, 1925, I gave you a check for $1,395?

13.   Isn't it true that this check of $1,395 represented the following items:

    1. $200 which you had gotten as a loan for me from your brother.

    2. $195 which I owed you.

    3.   A loan of $1,000 from me to you.

14.   Isn't it true that I took pity upon your financial condition and that I lent you the $1,000.

15.   Isn't it true that the Order Sons of Italy did not want to pay you any money and that you were in terrible financial straits and starving?

16.   Isn't it true that you asked the Order for money for your services and had not received any from the Order up to the 12th of November?

17.   Isnt it true that you desired to get some money for your servces to the Order from the Mieles, and that you did not succeed as usual, in your applications to the clan?

18.   Is it true or is it not true, that you have a hatred for the Miele clan, but that you stick together with them because you have a greater hatred of judge Cotillo?

19.   If the motive of Ferrari in now attacking Miele is that the Miele clan refused to let you have a loan for me, and refused also to lend you personally $200, which you asked them for, how do you account for the fact, if you deny that you have a pro-

found and unconfirmed hatred of judge Cotillo, that you are not attacking the Mieles?

20. Did you tell third parties, or any one else, since the breach between us, what I had done for you financially, intellectually and spiritually?

21. Have you ever referred since the break, to the deep debt you owe me for my association with you; and the moral prestige I gave you—you who were well known among the Italians for what you are—by my connection with you?

CHAPTER VIII.

I accuse

I charge the officers with neglect of principle.

I charge them with the neglect of ideas.

I charge them with lack of ideals.

I charge them with neglect of honorable opportunities for the Italian in the State of New York.

I charge them with a profound and everlasting hatred of individuals.

I charge them with the highest hypocrisy.

I charge them with doctoring the minutes.

I charge them with making it impossible for me to obtain a correct reflection in the minutes of what happened at the meetings.

I charge them with brutality, verbal and physical.

I charge them with preventing free discussion.

I charge them with miserliness and stinginess to employees and with wild extravagance with funds in connection with matters not pertaining to the Mortuary Fund.

I charge them with trying to make me a decorative figure.

I charge them with resisting my efforts to become independent of all trammels of outside men and independent of all shackles, except the shackles of law and morality.

I charge them with using upon me, at first blandishments and verbal caresses, to lead me to their desires.

I charge them, when blandishments and caresses failed, with the exertion of mental coercion and physical force.

I accuse them of charging to the Mortuary Fund expenses the Commission had not authorized.

I charge them with trying to make me an instrument and an accomplice of a gang of free-booters, who dominated the Order.

I charge Stephen Miele with conceit, with bombast and stupidity.

I charge him with venomous hate of individuals in the Sons of Italy Grand Lodge.

I charge him with the violation of law.

I charge him with underground practices in the Commission and out of the commission.

I charge him with taking advantage of his strategic position in the order to over-awe and impose his will upon weak and helpless commissioners and members of the Grand Council.

I charge him with tyrannizing over the Members of the Commission and of the Grand Council.

I charge him with the presentation of proposals to the Grand Council and the M. F., which were illegal and immoral.

I charge him with the inducement, the instigation of these members to violate, not only the laws of the Order but the general law of New York State, the moral law and the common rules of decent behavior in the society of men.

I charge him with preventing all amicable settlement of the case against the Sons of Italy Grand Lodge, by his nefarious and obstructive tactics after the Committee of Counsel for the plaintiff had discussed the provisions of an amicable settlement, at least pending the litigation and one lawyer had drawn up a tentatve operating agreement.

I charge him with influencing the Grand Venerable not to accept that agreement for specious and invalid and egotistical reasons.

I charge him with bearing deep and abiding hate against several individuals of the Sons of Italy Grand Lodge and particularly against Supreme Court Justice Salvatore A. Cotillo.

I charge him with endeavoring to draw me into this circle of venom and hate for his own purposes.

I charge him with endeavoring to get me to cross-examine Judge Cotillo, an endeavor which failed, and an endeavor which produced an immediate reaction by me, which Miele never forgot.

I charge him with the gravest hypocrisy.

I charge him with the most bare-faced shamelessness.

I charge him with the baseness of him who uses the basest weapons in combat.

I charge him with inventing the only defense that he has been able to conceive, a defense that even if true would not be used by decent, honorable men.

I charge the Miele clan with being in strategic positions in the Order, in the Supreme Council, in the Mortuary Fund and in the Grand Council for the purpose of controlling and dominating in every sphere of endeavor the Order Sons of Italy.

CHAPTER IX.

AFTERGLOW

Light in the Dark

Soft you; a word or two before you go,
I have done the State some service, and they know it;
No more of that. I pray you in your letters,
When you shall these unlucky deeds relate,
Speak of me as I am; nothing extenuate,
Nor set down aught in malice . . . . . .
     Set you down this;
And say besides, that in
     Aleppo once,
Where a malignant and a turbaned Turk
Beat a Venetian and traduced the State,
I took by the throat the circumcized dog,
     And smote him thus.—Othello.
In the calm lights of mild philosophy.—Addison.
There are more things in heaven and earth, Horatio,
Than are dreamt of in your philosophy.—Shakespeare.
There are no birds in last year's nest.—Longfellow.
Now all the youth of England are on fire,
And silken dalliance in the wardrobe lies.—Shakespeare.
And out of good still to find means of evil.—Milton.
Though fallen on evil days,
On evil days tho fallen, and evil tongues.—Ibid.
Will yet fertilize the soil tho' vanished.—Ibid.
   A Primrose by a river's brim
   A yellow primrose was to him,
   And it was nothing more.—Wadsworth.
Ring out the old, ring in the new.—Tennyson.
Ring out the old cause, and ancient forms of party strife.—Ibid.
A man that studieth revenge keeps his own wounds green,
   which otherwise would heal and do well.—Bacon.
   Revenge at first thought sweet,
   Bitter ere long back on itself recoils.—Milton.
Let's do it after the high Roman fashion.—Shakespeare.
     'Tis the last rose of summer
      Left blooming alone
     All her lovely companions
      Are faded and gone.—T. Moore.
    Gather ye rosebuds while ye may,
     Old Time is still aflying;
    And this same flower that smiles today
    Tomorrow will be dying.—Herrick.

Come unto these yellow sands.—Shakespeare.
Your old men shall dream dreams, your young men shall see visions.—Joel.
Yet I doubt not through the ages one increasing purpose runs,
And the thoughts of men are widened with the process of the suns.—Tennyson.

CHAPTER IX.

AFTERGLOW

Light in the Dark

—

I do not regret the experiences and the expense of time and money. It was worth a million to me in knowledge and in the fact that I need not repeat it or feel the desire to repeat it.

The knowledge I gained in six months or more of men and things of the Sons of Italy in America, is enough to furnish me with ammunition for the rest of my life.

Americans ought to know the conditions that exist in the Order Sons of Italy and that the persons who stand for the Order are not representative of it.

If the situation is not presented clearly and finally to the American public, the American public will get a wrong conception of the elevation and distinction of the Italians in America. Bad representatives of the races in this country have done an enormous amount of harm to the races they have misrepresented. Let the American public know that these men who stand forth are only the froth which has risen to the top and that they do not represent the substantial stuff of the Italians in America.

The white light of publicity that beats upon the Order will finally melt and dissolve the liquescent stuff which now maltreats and distorts the Order before the American public. The Italians need the help of the American public to take out of the Order the last cancers that are eating out its very heart.

The Italians in this country have a great future before them. That future ought not to be jeopardized by men, who infest the Order Sons of Italy at the present time. The reflection of Italian life cast upon the American scene, is a reflection full of deep shadows. The Order should be purified. Not only to benefit the Order itself and God knows it need purification, but primarily, to clear away the obstacles that are in the path of the Italians in this country. With polticians in the Order Sons of Italy, who desire to use the Order for their own aggrandizement and advancement and who are constantly plotting to have American politicians and American public men pull their chestnuts out of the fire, the Order is in a bad way. It is on the way to rapid destruction. With that destruction of the Order will come a repercussion upon the Italians of this country. But this repercussion on account of the destruction of the Order will be short-lived.

The best thing that could happen to the Italians in the United States, unless there is a clean sweep of the men, the practices and the methods in vogue, is the obliteration from Italian life of an Order that only degrades the Italians in the eyes of the Americans. Such an Order will delay and prevent the Americanization which all of us hope for and all of us ardently desire. The Italians must become part and parcel of the American public. They cannot become bone of bone and flesh of flesh of the American body politic unless they get rid of the false prophets who have misled them and unless they eradicate the shady methods that have hitherto obtained.

The Italians should be ashamed of themselves. From over three millions of Italians in the United States and over a million of Italians in the City of New York, it is difficult to get any harmony or concord of action in any useful or noble purpose. There are thousands of institutions necessary for the Italians but these institutions are not erected. There is too much desire of individuals to become prominent and there is too much personality. There is no submersion of the individual in the common good as there is in the case of other races in the United States. The Jews are just now in a campaign for the raising of fifteen million dollars, six million of which has to be raised in the City of New York. Within a very short time that fifteen millions will be raised. What could not the Italians do with $1,000,000. And yet, even if they were able to gather together one million dollars, there would be so much squabbling among the leaders and directors, that harmony of action would be paralyzed and nothing would be done with the money.

The most important thing for the Italians is to dash to pieces the leaders who have betrayed them, begin life anew with new men and change their psychology of inaction and suspicion to one of action and confidence in persons who deserve that confidence. The institutions the Italians need in this country will soon rise and will develop into the glory of the Italian colony and the hope of the country in which we live.

I see a vision of greatness for the Italians in this country—a vision which ought not to be delayed and cannot be allowed to be delayed.

There is a story that is read by every child in English speaking countries and that appeals with great drawing power to every grown up man. It is "Gulliver's Travels." Gulliver finds himself in the land of the Lilliputians. During his sleep he is bound with cords by these small men. The Lilliputians thought that they had bound the giant and made him helpless forever. But on awakening Gulliver breaks the cords with ease. The Italians are like the giant Gulliver. They are bound, shackled and fettered by themselves and by enemies outside the fold. But the cords are weak and the giant is strong. He is in repose. When he awakes he will break the cords that bind him, arise, stand upright, and march on to the conquest of his rightful position in America.

THE END.

APPENDIX 1.

This is the Title Page of and the Preface to the Memorandum referred to on page 13.

It shows how ardently I wanted unity and harmony and how balanced I tried to be even tho I was a combatant.

SUPREME COURT—STATE OF NEW YORK COUNTY OF ONEIDA.

SUPREME LODGE ORDER SONS OF ITALY IN AMERICA, INC., et al.,
Plaintiffs,

—against—

SONS OF ITALY GRAND LODGE, INC., et al.,
Defendants.

A REVIEW OF THE FACTS AND OF THE LAW
By
ROBERT FERRARI

Of Counsel for the Grand Lodge of the State of New York,
Order Sons of Italy in America, Inc.
and
President of the Mortuary Fund.

Published for the benefit of
The Emergency Mortuary Fund.

PREFACE.

The division in the Grand Lodge of the State of New York of the Order Sons of Italy in America, which took place on the 6ts day of August 1925, by the secession of the group calling itself Sons of Italy Grand Lodge which held a Convention in New York City, has caused great confusion in the minds of the members of the Order and strangers to the Order concerning the rights and the wrongs of the question.

Many members of the Order have written or phoned me, asking for information concerning the facts and the law and for my opinion. It is impossible to answer each individual.

There is a great deal of debate and discussion which is uncertain and unfounded. There is the difficulty of basing our arguments upon the facts; and there is the further difficulty of basing our arguments upon the law. There is the legal side to the question of which is the legitimate lodge, the lodge which met in Convention in New York City or the lodge which met in Convention in Schenectady under the auspices of the Supreme Lodge of the United States. There is further, the moral question involveld as to which Convention acted in accordance with the laws, the customs and the traditions of the Order. This moral question cinr.ot possibly be decided without recourse to the history of the matter and the facts in the case. The legal question cannot be resolved without recourse to the principles of law and the decisions of the Courts.

Speakers are constantly at a loss in going to the various subordinate lodges in this critical time when both sides desire the moral and the material support of the subordinate lodges, for the accurate facts in the complicated and involved history of this case; and for the proper principles of law and the decisions of the Courts to apply in the instant case. To these speakers it is hoped that the following pamphlet will be a boon.

The pamphlet is particularly intended for the rank and file of the membership of the Order Sons of Italy in America, both in the State of New York and in the various states of the Union. For the members of the Order in the State of New York it is of prime and vital importance because it is incumbent upon them to make the great decision. At present there are some individuals hovering over neutral ground, not knowing which way to turn. To this large mass of individuals desirous of knowing some of the elements of the case this booklet, it is hoped, will be of some use.

While there is no immediate finincial interest involved to the members of the Order outside the State of New York as there is in the case of members of the Order in the State of New York, the members of the Order outside the State who have, by the way, through their Grand Lodges, already expressed their sympathy for the struggles of the Schenectady group under the protection of the Supreme Lodge, are most vitally interested from the point of view of the solidarity and the unity of the Order in the United States. If secession can be accomplished in one state it can be accomplished in others. Instead of having a unified, strong, powerful Order all over the United States we shall have a series of separate entities which have lost their savor, their importance and their striking power.

I have made an attempt to be objective and impartial. I do not flatter myself that I have succeeded. It is very difficult at the easiest, to be both impartial and exact, especially when a person is involved in a struggle. But it has been my high endeavor to try to present the facts and the law to the best of my ability in as accurate and impartial a form as possible. I have therefore, not dealt with personalities. Nor have I dealt in denunciations and accusations. We have a question of principle here and not of personality. It does not matter who the individuals are. History has long life and individuals come and go. We are interested in maintaining and establishing a principle; and the individuals, if any, who have violated the principles count as nothing in the long and continuous flux of time.

Finally, I have attempted to give a series of points to be developed by the reader himself instead of an elaborate discussion of the points themselves. This pamphlet could easily have been expanded into a book. But who would have read the book? In this time of hurry and bustle, even men of leisure and inclination find it difficult to wade through a tome of several hundred pages. I should rather give the reader credit for intelligence and for the ability to develop the points made by the author. The amplifications, with good will, can easily be made. There must, in addition, be considered the fact that the whole view of the argument can be gotten more comprehensively and more completely when the case is put into brief form.

The place set by the Yonkers Convention of the Grand Lodge of the State of New York in 1924, for the Convention of 1925, was Schenectady. This was in accordance with the Constitution and By-Laws of the Order.

On the 20th day of July 1925, the members of the Order were notified that the Convention of the Grand Lodge would be held in Schenectady according to the decision of the last Convention of the Grand Lodge. On July 1925 the Grand Venerable notified the **delegates that the Convention would not be held in Schenectady but** in New York. A group of delegates and members of the Order objected to the transference of the Convention Seat to New York and appealed to the Supreme Lodge to hold the meeting of the Grand Lodge of the State of New York under the auspices of the Supreme Lodge at the place designated by the Convention of 1924. This produced confusion worse confounded, in the ranks of the Order in New York State. Some delegates went to the New York Convention and some delegates went to the Schenectady Convention.

The funds of the Order were in possession of the group that

met in New York City; and the machinery of administration per-
fected by many years of labor, was at their disposal. The Schenectady group had to create a system of government for the administration of the affairs of the Grand Lodge. It had to set up new machinery for administration, a new organization;and temporary and
immediate means for launching the new enterprise. Among the
means employed for floating the new organization was that of an
Emergency Mortuary Fund. The Mortuary Fund of the Order is a
thing which is nearest to the hearts of members; and it was natural
therefore, that the Schenectady group should provide some means for
collecting a fund out of which death benefits could be paid so that no
beneficiaries of members of the Order should suffer. The plan hit
upon was the following:

Lodges which had not yet paid the monthly assessment should
pay that monthly assessment to the Grand Lodge, to form the nucleus
of a reserve fund; and the members of the Subordinate Lodges who
remained faithful to the Order should make a voluntary loan of one
dollar a member. This fund might be used for the expenses of
adadministration at the beginning of the difficult task set the Mortuary Commission. Within one month after setting up the machinery
of the Mortuary Fund two thousand dollars were paid out to the
beneficiaries of five deceased members, without calling upon the members who remained with the Schenectady group for any assessment
as is usual and normal according to the Constitution and By-Laws of
the Order.

Division in the State of New York has temporarily set back the
movement for the solidification and the unification of the Italian
strength in the United States. If this modest effort can help in any
way to revive and invigorate the Order throughout the United States,
the author and the Mortuary Commission for itself, for the Order,
and specifically for the Emergency Mortuary Fund of the Schenectady
group, will have considered their labors and their pains well spent.

ROBERT FERRARI.

APPENDIX 2.

This is the table of contents of the Memorandum of 47 pages mentioned on page 13.

TABLE OF CONTENTS.

APPENDIX 3.

February 15, 1926.

Mr. Francis J. Panetta, Order Sons of Italy,
27 Cleveland Place, — New York City.
Dear Frank:

I have received your message telling me that a committee of the Grand Council would like to wait upon me.

I have the utmost respect for the committee of the Grand Council but no useful purpose can be served by my meeting them. I dislike to rake over dying members.

Let them die.

My decision is irrevocable.

I have also resigned from the Order Sons of Italy in America.

With kindest personal regards, I am, cordially yours,

ROBERT FERRARI.

APPENDIX 4.

Mr. Luigi Sardi, 1042 40th Street,   July 31, 1925.

Brooklyn, New York.

Dear Brother Sardi:

Will you be good enough to come to my office at 5 o'clock Monday afternoon to meet Brother Siani, our secretary and me to talk over matters pertaining to our Order.

With kind personal regards and with eagerness to see you, I am
RF/RJ   Cordially yours,

Hon. John J. Freschi,   February 3, 1926.

Grand Venerable of the State of New York,

Order Sons of Italy in America,

50 Pine Street, New York City.

Dear Grand Venerable Freschi:

I resign from the position of President of the Mortuary Fund of the Grand Lodge of the State of New York, Order Sons of Italy of America.

I withdraw as counsel to the Grand Lodge of the State of New York, Order Sons of Italy in America.

Both resignations to take effect immediately.

With my best personal regards, I am,
RF/RJ   Cordially yours,

Mr. Louis Sardi,   February 3, 1926.

Venerable of the Lodge "Fratelli Uniti,"

1042 40th Street, Brooklyn, N. Y.

Dear Brother Sardi:

I resign from membership in the Lodge, "Fratelli Uniti."

RF/RJ   Sincerely yours,

APPENDIX 5.

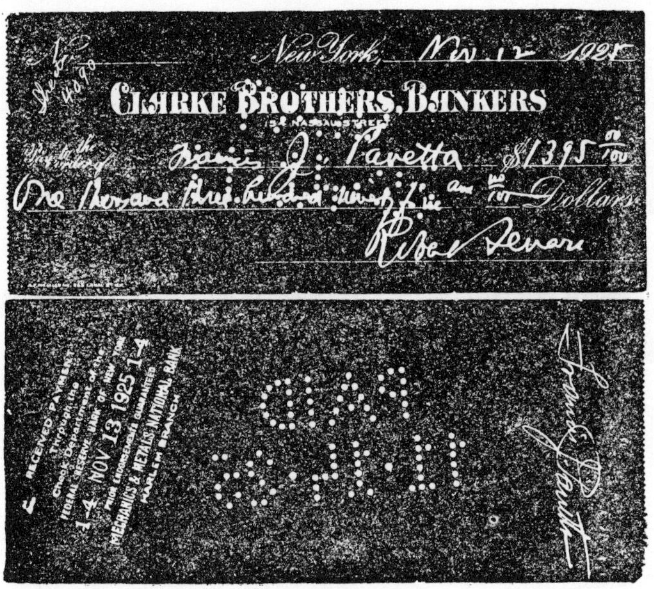

APPENDIX 6.

Mr. Mario De Pasquale,   September 17, 1925.
Sect'y Mortuary Fund,
27 Cleveland Place,
New York City.
Dear Brother De Pasquale:

When the minutes of the committee meeting are drawn up will you kindly tell Trapani to have two typewritten copies made, one for the files and one for myself.

I hope to see you on your return from your trip.

Cordially and fraternally yours,

RF/RJ

Mr. Trapani,   December 31, 1925.
Order Sons of Italy,
27 Cleveland Place,
New York City.
Dear Trapani:

Please order from Brother Capparelli, 150 copies of the last two issues of the Vessillo, and 150 of the coming issue and arrange with me to send them to the delegates at the Schenectady convention and to the Venerables of the various Lodges.

Cordially and fraternally yours,

RF/RJ

P. S. I do not wish the Mortuary Fund to stand for this expense. I shall pay for it myself. Please communicate with me as to the best means of sending them and as to the persons to send them to.

INDEX.

INDEX

DAYS PLEASANT AND UNPLEASANT

in the

ORDER SONS OF ITALY IN AMERICA

The Problem of Races and Racial Societies in the United States

Assimilation or Isolation?

by

ROBERT FERRARI

GIORNI DI PIACERE E DISGUSTO

passati nell'Ordine Figli d'Italia in America

dal Maggio 1925 al Febbraio 1926

di

ROBERT FERRARI

MANDY PRESS, Inc.
30 Park Place
New York

INDICE DELLE MATERIE

PREFAZIONE

Il discutere è già per sè stesso interessante. Tanto più interessante, quando si aggira intorno a grandi principi. La questione dell'isolamento o dell'assimilazione, in questo paese, dei gruppi stranieri, è la più urgente ed in pari tempo la perenne questione della nostra vita, fino a quando non sarà adeguatamente risoluta.

Questo volumetto mira a trattare tale argomento a vantaggio della vita attuale e della vita futura di questo paese — vita attuale e futura indissolubilmente connessa con la esatta soluzione del problema delle razze e delle reciproche relazioni fra loro.

Il lettore però non troverà discussioni astratte.

Abbiamo finora subite troppe discussioni aeriformi, senza l'indicazione di uno luogo o di un nome. Qui le conclusioni sono brevi concrete ed evidenti, ed il ragionamento su cui si basano è tratto dalla vita attuale vissuta e da fatti realmente avvenuti. I fatti che ebbero luogo durante il mio esperimento quale ufficiale della più grande società italiana negli Stati Uniti.

Dicono che nell'Ordine Figli d'Italia si raccolgano 300,000 membri. Negli Stati Uniti gli Italiani sono 3.000.000. Direttamente o indirettamente, quindi, l'Ordine riguarda quasi ogni italiano residente in America, sia nato in questo paese, sia immigrato.

E' opportuno, perciò, iniziare una pubblica discussione intorno agli effetti di quest'Ordine o simiglianti Ordini e Società, esistenti negli Stati Uniti, per studiare in qual modo influiscono sulle stesse Associazioni e sui membri di queste, ed in qual modo individui ed associazioni si riverberano sul complesso della politica americana.

La mia conclusione è contraria a questi agglomerati che pervertono e ritardano l'assimilazione con gli americani.

Il grave pericolo consiste che, come durante la guerra, i governanti della Nazione, possano commettere l'errore fatale di imporre con la forza la coltura e l'assimilazione; gettando così la giovane generazione fra le braccia dei naturali nemici — gli elementi, cioè, contrari all'assimilazioni ed i fautori dell'isolamento.

L'argomento è alto.

La mia speranza è che sia stato trattato elevatamente.

ROBERTO FERRARI

INTRODUZIONE

Entrai nell'Ordine nel Febbraio 1926, pensando che avrei potuto essere utile a questo ed agli Italiani immigrati negli Stati Uniti e con essi alla mia terra d'origine.

Mi ero sempre tenuto lontano dalle Società Italiane ed avevo vissuta una vita di lavoro fra gli amici americani d'ogni razza.

Una scissura nell'Ordine ebbe luogo nel mese di Luglio 1926. Un gruppo si adunò a New York. L'altro gruppo si adunò a Schenectaday. Io andai a Schenectaday. Fui eletto Presidente del Fondo Mortuario; un fondo che avea raggiunto la somma di $200.000.

Arrivati a New York, il 9 di Agosto, cominciammo ad organizzare il funzionamento. Sorsero immediatamente difficoltà fra me e gli ufficiali. Si determinò l'urto fra i diversi temperamenti tradizioni ed esperienze. Una serie di contrasti, che sono dettagliati nelle pagine seguenti, condussero alla crisi che ebbe luogo nell'adunanza del 12 Gennaio 1926 quando una condotta villana insieme a metodi illegali giunsero sino all'apice della tolleranza.

Fui pressato a fare un prestito sul fondo pei defunti, affidati alla Commissione che presiedevo, per pagare degli avvocati ingaggiati in una lite pendente fra i due gruppi sopra menzionati. Rifiutai. Subito dopo mi dimisi da Presidente del Fondo Mortuario, da avvocato della Grande Loggia dello Stato di New York e da membro dell'Ordine. Il mio disgusto era profondo.

Credetti che sarei stato lasciato in pace ad attendere ai miei affari. Feci il conto senza l'oste. Le mie dimissioni aveano prodotto la rivoluzione nelle file. La massa desiderava sapere per quali ragioni me n'ero andato. L'Ordine si trovò nella necessità di soddisfare tal desiderio.

Due mesi dopo le mie dimissioni apparve nei giornali italiani un Comunicato del Fondo Mortuario, compilato ed espresso in modo da significare che io avevo abbandonato l'Ordine per ragioni personali e non a causa del modo come esso era condotto ed amministrato; aggiungendo che io avevo firmato un check di $2.500 con cui fare un prestito al Grande Concilio del nostro gruppo, per pagare la parte del compenso agli Avvocati, spettante allo Stato di New York. Si faceva intendere implicitamente che io avevo votato pel prestito. Invece io avevo votato contro.

Risposi a mezzo di un intervista concessa ad Ernesto Valentini, uno dei migliori giornalisti in America. La discussione si protrasse oltre un mese — avendo gli ufficiali del mio gruppo asserito le cose più pazze e stravaganti.

Io ero costretto innanzi tutto ad attendere ai miei affari professionali, per cui non potevo seguire questa gente in una guerriglia in cui sono sperimentati maestri e per cui aveano a disposizione lunghe ore d'ozio. Il fradiciume veniva a galla. Essi sono insuperabili nel maneggiare il fango. Decisi di rispondere a tutto ed a tutti e stabilire i fatti dei miei rapporti con l'Ordine. Da ciò questo libro. Hinc illae lacrymae. Da ciò le loro lacrime.

GIORNI DI PIACERE E DISGUSTO
passati nell'Ordine Figli d'Italia in America
dal Maggio 1925 al 3 Febbraio 1926

Una Commedia dal titolo

LA NOBILE BANDA

Personaggi: Distribuzioni delle parti:

Il Grande Concilio Esecutivo — La Commissione del Fondo Unico Mortuario, con i nomi dei componenti, riportati nella parte in inglese e comprensibili, anche, da chi non conosce la lingua.

Carattere dei Personaggi
e premonizione della natura di ciascuno di essi

fatta a mezzo di citazioni, proverbi, passi, e sentenze di personaggi e scrittori, come Pope — Moore — Adam Smith — Shakspeare — Samuel Johnson — Tennyson — Milton — Holmes — Byron — Kipling — Wordsworth — Dryden — Thompson — Lanier — Young Scott — Gibbon — Lowell.

Del Grande Concilio Esecutivo è detto fra l'altro:
"Il Dritto divino dei re di sgovernare" — Pope.

Di Stefano Miele è detto:
"Un falso viso deve nascondere ciò che la falsa anima conosce" —
Shakspeare

Di Panetta: "Ingrato, fedifrago, odiatore non è questo un Giuda in larga scala" — Holmes.

Di Robert Ferrari: "E' pericoloso stuzzicare un nido di vespe" —
Dryden.

Di Capparelli: "Dopo andò a letto e dormi profondamente, come se avesse pagato una cambiale" — Lanier.

Lavoro compiuto da me quale avvocato della Gran Loggia, nella causa dell'Ordine dei Figli d'Italia in America, contro i Sons of Italy Grand Lodge.

Quattro settimane di meetings, quasi giornalieri, della durata di tre a sei ore ciascuno.

Tre memorandum intorno ai fatti ed al diritto della causa, presentati il 12 e 17 Agosto e 7 Settembre.

Oltre a numerosi convegni con avvocati e non avvocati per discutere fatti e prove legali; oltre ad infinite ricerche di giurisprudenza; oltre a consigli legali dati a centinaia di persone connesse con le Logge, col Fondo Mortuario, col Grande, nonchè col Supremo Concilio.

Scrissi una guida, contenente i principi direttivi per le Logge subordinate e la Grande Loggia.

Il 1 Settembre 1925 difesi una causa a Oyster Bay, di cui il "Nuovo Vessillo" riferì il 12 Settembre.

Memorandum, Sunti ed Articoli scritti da Robert Ferrari.

"Nuovo Vessillo", Dicembre 1925 a Gennaio 1926; Articolo in 6 puntate; I Figli d'Italia. Una Storia. 10.000 parole.

Dicembre, 1925; Articolo: "La Funzione e l'Avvenire degli Italiani negli Stati Uniti".

Dicembre, 1925; Articoli sul "Fondo Unico Mortuario".

Scritti Legali — Un Memorandum di 10 pagine; 2 cause, 47 pagine.

Discorsi riportati: nel "Nuovo Vessillo" 17 Ottobre 1925 e "Corriere d'America" 6 Ottobre 1925.

CRONOLOGIA DEGLI EVENTI

1. Entrai nell'Ordine il 14 Maggio 1925.

2. Eletto dalla mia Loggia, Fratelli Uniti, delegato supplente alla Convenzione della Grande Loggia, l'11 Giugno 1925.

3. Presi parte alla Convenzione di Schenectady dal 5 all'8 Agosto 1925.

4. Aprile 6, secessione dalla Grande Loggia Ordine Figli d'Italia, in America, dei Sons of Italy che tennero la Convenzione nella città di New York.

5. Sono eletto presidente del Fondo Unico Mortuario del Gruppo di Schenectady.

6. Sono nominato avvocato della Grande Loggia del Gruppo di Schenectady.

7. Adunanze mensili fino al 14 Dicembre 1925 del F. U. M.

8. Adunanza in cui avvenne la crisi — 12 Gennaio 1926.

9. Gennaio 15, 1926 — Adunanza riunita del Grande Concilio e della Commissione del F. U. M.

10. Gennaio 22, 1926 — Adunanza della Commissione F. U. M. con l'intervento degli up-state men.

11. Gennaio 29, 1926 — Adunanza della Commissione del F. U. M. nella quale venne votato il prestito di 2.500 pel pagamento degli onorari agli avvocati, su raccomandazione del Grande Concilio fatta alla Commissione F. U. M.

CRONOLOGIA DELLA CONTROVERSIA
fra il Grande Concilio, la Commissione del Fondo Unico Mortuario e Roberto Ferrari

Dopo le dimissioni del 3 Febbraio 1926, al 19 Aprile 1926.

Febbraio 3, 1926 — Dimissioni di Roberto Ferrari da Presidente del F. U. M. Ritiro dalla difesa della Gran Loggia; e dimissioni dalla Loggia Fratelli Uniti.

Marzo 28, 1926 — Adunanza del Grande Concilio e della Commissione F. U. M. per decidere sulle comunicazioni da inviare alla stampa a riguardo delle dimissioni di Roberto Ferrari.

Marzo 29, 1926 — Prima comunicazione alla stampa del Segretario del Fondo Mortuario autorizzata dal Grande Concilio e dal Fondo Unico Mortuario.

Arile 6, 1926 — Mia risposta — Intervista col "Nuovo Mondo"

Aprile 7, 1926 — Dichiarazione di Roberto Ferrari nel "Nuovo Mondo" e nella "Follia".

Aprile 16, 1926 — Lettera del Grande Concilio alla stampa rispondente alla mia dichiarazione ed all'intervista del 6 Aprile.

Aprile 19, 1926 — Circolare 21, contenente la comunicazione alla stampa del 16 Aprile con l'aggiunta di un introduzione.

Seconda Intervista pubblicata nel "Nuovo Mondo" 25 Aprile

Aprile 26, 1926 — Comunicazione alla stampa del F. U. M. pubblicata nel "Corriere d'America".

Maggio 4, 6 e 7, 1926 — Risposta al comunicato del F. U. M. dell'Aprile 26, nel "Nuovo Mondo".

CRONOLOGIA DEGLI EVENTI

Date delle lettere fra me, il Segretario, altri membri della Commissione ed il Grande Venerabile e sommario di queste lettere.

Ottobre 6, 1925 — Ipersensibilità del Segretario della Commissione. Il Segretario si lamenta per avere io lodato il Segretario del Grande Concilio. Rispondo.

Agosto 31, 1925 — Lettera al vice-segretario, chiedente ogni giorno notizie e condizioni del fondo e quel che accadeva in ufficio.

Ottobre 8, 1925 — Lettera di ringraziamento all'Editore del "Corriere" per aver pubblicato il mio comunicato intorno ai diritti dei combattenti e dei neutri — una lettera tendente a mantenere l'equilibrio tra le parti, malgrado la mia partecipazione alla lotta, e stabilire nell'Ordine i diritti della massa che era la più danneggiata pei dissidi dei capi.

Novembre 4, 1925 — Lettera al vice-segretario, il quale desiderava mostrarmi tutto quanto era destinato alla pubblicazione, e si duoleva per una comunicazione della Commissione alla stampa, apparsa il 4 Novembre.

Novembre 6, 1925 — Lettera al Segretario riguardante due sussidi per morte, presentati alla Commissione, ed in cui si davano le ragioni per cui non si agiva sulla base dei documenti sottomessi.

Decembre 18, 1925 — Lettera al Segretario deplorante l'incuria dei verbali, ed il pagamento, da parte della Commissione, di servizi non autorizzati.

Decembre 18, 1925 — Lettera al vice-segretario chiedendogli di venire al mio ufficio per mostrarmi tutti i bills, lettere e circolari scritte dai membri della Commissione o dagli impiegati.

Gennaio 11, 1926 — Lettera al Segretario deplorante l'inesattezza dei verbali nel riferire le mie obiezioni alla concessione del prestito di $2.500. Il mio lamento concerneva pure la discrepanza fra il verbale e quanto era avvenuto nella Commissione in riguardo a l'Ospedale Italiano.

Gennaio 19, 1926 — Lettera al vice-segretario del Gran Concilio, a riguardo dell'adunanza del 22 Gennaio.

Gennaio 28, 1926 — Lettera al Grande Venerabile esprimente il desiderio di dimettermi.

Febbraio 3, 1926 — Lettera al Venerabile della Loggia subordinata "Fratelli Uniti" per dimettermi dalla Loggia.

Febbraio 3, 1926 — Lettera al Grande Venerabile di dimissione da Presidente del F. U. M. e da avvocato della Grande Loggia.

CRONOLOGIA DELLA "PRESIDENZA ONORARIA"
di STEFANO MIELE

Gennaio 5, 1926 — Circolare 15 del Grande Concilio. Vi appare il suo nome quale Presidente Onorario.

Febbraio 10, 1926 — Circolare No. 17. Il suo nome è cancellato.

CAPITOLO I.

LA FIAMMA

FATTI ED ARGOMENTI

Per coloro i quali non fossero forti nella lingua inglese sono riassunti qui in una sintesi scheletrica i fatti esposti da Roberto Ferrari in inglese.

Non troverete l'eloquenza e la forza polemica di Ferrari, ma avrete la sequenza logica e cronologica dei fatti, su cui ogni lettore potrà formare un giudizio.

La Circolare No. 21 della Gran Loggia dello Stato di New York, Ordine Figli d'Italia, in America, 27 Cleveland Place, contiene una lettera, che intende rispondere al mio comunicato alla stampa e ad un intervista avuta con Ernesto Valentini.

L'introduzione alla lettera mi da occasione di rispondere alle accuse lanciate contro di me, non solo, ma di far la storia dei miei rapporti con l'Ordine dei Figli d'Italia in America.

Dopo le mie dimissioni del 3 Febbraio 1926 rimasi per due mesi silenzioso, malgrado venissi da più parti incitato a parlare.

Il fatto che mi dimisi il 3 Febbraio non deve far credere che le ragioni che mi indussero a separarmi dall'Ordine, si siano verificate proprio in quel giorno.

Fu appena ebbi cominciato a funzionare da Presidente del Fondo Unico Mortuario che mi convinsi di essere fuori posto.

Mi occorreva una ragione plausibile per uscire con onore e dignità. Dovevo giustificare al pubblico l'abbandono.

Fortunatamente per me, e per chi si interessa dell'Ordine, rimasi in esso 6 mesi, abbastanza cioè per osservare ed informarmi sullo stato degli affari e sugli uomini, in modo da discuterli con diretta conoscenza.

Ora posso affermare e dimostrare che i dirigenti e dominatori dell'Ordine sono indegni del rispetto degli Italiani negli Stati Uniti.

La Circolare No. 21 nella introduzione afferma molte cose, che coloro i quali le diffusero sanno essere false.

Non posso credere che Freschi, Angrisani, o i membri del Gran Concilio dell'up-state, conobbero il contenuto della circolare, prima della pubblicazione. Probabilmente essa è opera della "gang" che voleva imporsi anche a me, e che impose loro la circolare.

Ma, è ora più d'una settimana, dacchè essa fu pubblicata, ed ancora non è stata ripudiata da nessuno. E' possibile che l'Ordine, a causa degli individui che lo dirigono, eserciti una influenza deleteria e contaminatrice su tutti coloro che con esso hanno contatti?

Da ciò che ho veduto, da ciò che ho udito sono più che mai convinto, che questi dominatori dell'Ordine devono rimanere uniti e volendo riuscire ad ogni costo nei loro intenti, usano ogni arma non importa quanto bassa o vile.

In questa Circolare essi cantano la stessa canzone, che intonano ogni qualvolta qualcuno tenti di far qualcosa per l'Ordine, e ne fu impedito con imposizioni e maltrattamenti da parte dei nemici che l'Ordine ha nel seno.

Elevano il grido contro la tirannide, non la loro tirannide, ma la mia. Io che, da Presidente del F. U. M. permisi la massima libertà di espressione e di azione.

Sono imbestialiti perchè l'opposizione ha pubblicato i miei comunicati ed interviste.

Ma io detti le dimissioni senza dare una sola ragione. Ciò facendo volli, per un senso di delicatezza, impedire che le accuse da me formulate contro i capi dell'Ordine privatamente, venissero usate dagli avversari.

Ed ecco che mi si fa un carico di non avere addotto i motivi delle dimissioni.

Rimasi muto due mesi.

Ma quando, nella seconda metà di Marzo, apparve nei giornali un comunicato, in cui dicevasi che le dimissioni non erano state originate da ragioni generali riguardanti l'Amministrazione dell'Ordine, ma da ragioni personali; quando si faceva credere che io non solo avevo firmato il check di $2.500 da pagarsi dal F. U. M. per gli avvocati, ma che avevo votato in favore di tale concessione, mi fu reso impossibile continuare a tacere.

Fu allora che parlai. Fu da allora che vado parlando e continuerò a parlare, fino a quando Miele, l'individuo che domina l'Ordine, e nell'Ordine domina le persone, non verrà rovesciato dal piedestallo e l'Ordine non passerà in mani più degne.

Dicono di avermi elevato, benchè sconosciuto, ad un alta posizione dell'Ordine, ma non confessano che tale elevazione era a tutto loro ventaggio e non a mio. Non dicono che mi pregarono insistentemente perchè accettassi quel posto, che avevo già rifiutato come avevo rifiutato quello di Grande Oratore.

Andai a Schenectady senza chieder nulla. Infatti fino all'ultimo momento della partenza del battello non avevo deciso di andare. Prima della Convenzione ebbero luogo parecchie adunanze al Pennsylvania

Hotel del gruppo che rimase fedele alla Suprema Loggia, ma io non intervenni, intendendo rimaner neutro.

Furono alcuni eventi, nei quali non ebbero parte nessuno di coloro che andarono a Schenectady, e certi telegrammi e documenti pubblicati all'ultimo momento, e che lessi la notte del 4 Agosto che mi decisero a prendere il battello per Albany.

Non vi conoscevo più di tre o quattro persone. Non credo di avere avuto in tutto l'Ordine una dozzina di amici. Uno che conoscevo mi pose in rapporto con altri nel battello. Fui sollecitato a far parte di comitati, e per quattro giorni lavorai giorno e notte.

Io pensavo fosse meglio per me restar fuori d'ogni carica. Rifiutai la presidenza del F. U. M. Ma quando vidi che aveano assolutamente bisogno di uomini nuovi, fini per accettare.

Tentarono di usarmi, di trar vantaggio della mia reputazione guadagnata duramente, del prestigio del mio nome onesto, pei loro fini. Ma si accorsero di non potermi dominare. L'urto era inevitabile.

Ci vollero quattro mesi perchè venisse in discussione dinanzi alla Commissione l'importante argomento del prestito di $2.500 e l'altro di $1.700 per sopperire alle spese dei Grandi Delegati di Washington. Ce ne vollero altri due per risolvere finalmente la questione della mia permanenza nell'Ordine o della mia uscita. Ero stato nell'Ordine solo tre mesi prima della Convenzione e quindi ammetto che ero sconosciuto nell'Ordine. Ma questo distrugge l'asserzione che mi fossi aggregato ai Figli d'Italia per desiderio di pubblicità. Se ero sconosciuto che cosa potevo sperare?

Che pensare d'un Grande Concilio così idiota da pubblicare per le stampe la castroneria che io abbia in varie occasioni confessato d'essere entrato nell'Ordine per farmi una reclame, di cui avevo bisogno.

A chi mai dissi questo? Non certo ad uno del Concilio. Se confessai ciò a qualcun altro perchè il Gran Concilio non fa il nome?

Io avevo bisogno della pubblicità dei Figli d'Italia? Quando solo pochi mesi prima della Convenzione di Agosto, avevo avuto, col processo Ely, una reclame, nei più grandi giornali americani, che nessun membro del Gran Concilio e neppure tutto l'intero Grand Concilio, fu in grado mai avere.

Sono un positivista in politica, e non esito un momento a dire che desidererei aver controllo delle condizioni, per potere concretare le mie idee. Non esito a dire che quando entrai nell'Ordine mi facevo delle illusioni; che queste illusioni derivavano dal fatto che ignoravo gli uomini che dirigevano l'Ordine. Io infatti credevo che qualcosa potesse farsi di questa organizzazione, in modo da renderla un esponente degli Italiani ed una forza fra essi e fra le Comunità in cui essi vivono. Ciò non è biasimevole .

Mi accusano di essere un metafisico restio alla pratica della vita. Ma se non fossi stato un metafisico non avrei potuto usare loro, come essi pensavano di usar me. Ora essi sanno che quando un metafisico viene a contatto con un uomo pratico, rappresenta un grave pericolo.

Dicono, che volevo distruggere ogni autorità dell'Ordine. Se avessi fatto ciò, o se lo avessi desiderato non sarebbe stato un errore. Quando il potere che dirige è infetto non vi è ragione di rispettarlo

La tirannia di cui mi accusano non era che la mia tenace opposizione alle loro porcherie.

Mi opposi a molte cose che essi volevano fare.

Mi opposi energicamente alla concessione dei due prestiti perchè erano ingiusti, irregolari, illegali ed immorali.

Dicono, che non avevo programma sociale o culturale, che non l'ho mai accennato, serbandolo nel cervello, per paura qualcuno mi rubasse i diritti di autore.

Membri del Gran Consiglio erano presenti quando svolsi il mio programma sociale e culturale, e quando esposi le idee intorno all'opera degli Italiani negli Stati Uniti. Ho scritto pure degli articoli. Se i membri del Gran Concilio non li hanno letti potrò indicare ove furono stampati. Il "Corriere d'America" del 16 Ottobre 1925, contiene un breve resoconto d'una conferenza pronunziata nell'Ottobre 1925, all'inaugurazione della Loggia Nicola Misasi, nell'aula dei Figli d'Italia, East 15 Strade. Anche il "Nuovo Vessillo" del 17 Ottobre 1925 riportò un più largo resoconto.

Scrissi un articolo intitolato "I Figli d'Italia. Una storia" in cui esposi un programma sociale e culturale, indicando i problemi che l'ordine dovrebbe risolvere nella Comunità Americana, ed il miglior modo di risolverli. Questo articolo fu pubblicato in sei puntate nel "Nuovo Vessillo" da Dicembre 1925 a Gennaio 1926.

Insistetti sul bisogno per gli italiani di essere uniti, deplorando la scissione dell'Ordine.

Richiamo l'attenzione anche sull'articolo "Le funzioni e l'avvenire degli Italiani in America" nel "Nuovo Vessillo" del Dicembre 1925; nonchè sulla lettera, diretta al signor Garbellano, in cui parlavo del bisogno urgente di unità fra gli italiani in America, e delle funzioni che potrebbero compiere a mezzo dell'Ordine, se ben diretto.

CAPITOLO II.

IL MEETING DELLA CRISI, 12 GENNAIO 1926

Quanto finora fu detto, può non apparire a taluno sufficiente ragione della mia rivolta contro l'uomo che è il maggiore colpevole. Dev'esservi qualche ragione naturale che mi forza ad attaccar Miele, lo spirito malefico dell'Ordine.

Ebbi con lui per quindici anni una superficiale conoscenza di saluto. Non credo d'aver scambiato con lui più di cinquanta parole, durante il tempo che lo conosco.

Nei primi mesi i Miele usarono meco blandizie e carezze verbali. Quando videro che queste erano inutili, ricorsero alle coercizioni morali ed alla forza fisica. Dapprima Pasquale Miele parlò d'un banchetto con un anello di brillanti che mi sarebbe stato offerto. Lo stesso Stefano Miele, in presenza di Panetta, mi prospetto il successo finanziario e professionale che avrei conseguito con l'aiuto dell'Ordine. Risi d'un riso ironico e silenzioso in ambo i casi, ammirando, come dissi a Panetta, la stupidaggine di chi con siffatti discorsi credea influenzarmi.

Venni in contatto coi membri del Fondo Mortuario e del Gran Concilio e Miele era onnipresente. Così è che, mio malgrado, dovetti avere con lui più frequenti relazioni nelle quali, però, se usavo le forme usuali esteriori della considerazione, mi studiavo tenerlo a distanza.

Infatti egli capi, o gli fu detto, che mi ripugnava.

La differenza di concetti di metodi e di azione, fra noi, si era palesata.

Il 12 Gennaio ebbe luogo il meeting che ho denominato il meeting della crisi.

Miele, dinanzi al Gran Concilio, aveva, il 14 Dicembre 1925, per la prima volta presentata la proposta del prestito di $2,500.

Io mi opposi per le ragioni indicate nella lettera dell'11 Gennaio al Segretario della Commissione. Il 14 Dicembre fu la prima volta che sentii parlare del prestito, quantunque fosse stato deciso in un meeting del Supremo Concilio, in cui erano intervenuti i Grandi Venerabili di vari Stati, inclusi Freschi e Miele, naturalmente questi insieme a Freschi avevano deciso di domandare il prestito al Fondo Mortuario.

Io non ero stato consultato.

Differenze di temperamento ed intrighi di retroscena aveano prodotto il loro effetto, ed io non intervenivo così assiduamente alle adunanze, per cui Miele faceva tutto. Così fu che solo il 14 Dicembre ebbi notizia che si voleva un prestito dal fondo mortuario.

Quando Miele venne a richiederlo, consultai uno per uno tutti i Commissari, senza esprimere la mia opinione per non influenzarli. Erano tutti favorevoli. Dovetti spiegare le ragioni che mi facevano essere contrario.

A causa dell'atteggiamento di Miele verso di me e dei susurri intorno alla mia antipatia per lui, che, notisi, era cominciata sin dall'Agosto, cercai mantenere fra la Commissione e l'Ordine la maggiore armonia, pensando che dal momento che mi trovavo in quella orribile situazione, dovevo cavarne il miglior vantaggio possibile per l'Ordine.

Discussi le obiezioni al prestito con calma e serenità, che mi cattivarono la simpatia degli altri membri della Commissione, la quale decise di rimandare la decisione ad un altra adunanza per lasciarmi agio di meglio investigare.

Nei giorni dopo il meeting del 14 Dicembre, investigai e studiai, ma per venire alla conclusione, che il prestito era altamente illegale, e non poteva, sotto qualunque circostanza, esser concesso, non importa quanto vitale fosse la causa per cui si reclamava, e quanto forte la pressione di Miele e della sua banda per ottenerlo.

Ebbi poi personalmente piena e chiara l'impressione che Miele, e gli altri volevano il prestito, intendevano sporcamente abusare di me, nella mia posizione di Presidente del Fondo Mortuario, costringendomi ad un prestito che si riduceva ad una criminosa distruzione di fondi, destinati a ben diverso scopo.

La responsabilità morale e legale dell'atto era mia, e della Commissione, e non del Gran Concilio o del Grande Venerabile, che istigavano all'illegalità.

Ciò era affatto indifferente per Stefano Miele, abituato a metodi sotterranei e loschi, e che disse, in piena adunanza del 12 Gennaio, nulla di illegale o di immorale lo avrebbe arrestato dal fare quello che egli considerava vantaggioso alla posizione assunta. La sua lunga storia nell'Ordine ha spento, in lui, ogni senso di decenza. A lui importa poco rovinare l'Ordine, e coinvolgere, nella ruina, gente che avea mantenuta immacolata la reputazione. Egli non ha nulla da perdere. Ha già tutto perduto.

Spiegai la mia irrevocabile decisione agli ufficiali del Gran Concilio ed ai membri del Fondo Mortuario, e mi spinsi persino a dir loro che avevo consultato un autorevole avvocato, che non nomino. Non convocai, quindi, nessun'adunanza speciale dopo quella del 14 Dicembre. Attesi l'ordinaria riunione del 12 Gennaio, quando credevo che l'affare del prestito non sarebbe stato più riproposto.

Avevo fatto i conti senza l'oste.

Benchè il giorno 11 Gennaio avessi scritto al segretario lamentando che l'affare del prestito appariva nell'ordine del giorno, che ero inalterabilmente opposto ad esso, e desideravo venisse cancellato dall'ordine del giorno, la faccenda venne dinanzi alla Commissione e Miele era nuovamente là a sostenerla.

Dopo che io, invece di tagliar la discussione, permisi a tutti, incluso Miele, di parlare, quando volli ripetere gli argomenti contrari corroborati da tutto ciò che avevo raccolto lungo un mese di esame, Miele mi tagliò bruscamente la parola dicendo, essere inutile parlare sulla cosa, ed io avrei potuto fare quel che volevo.

CAPITOLI III. e IV.

L'AZIONE PRECIPITA SINO ALLO SVOLGIMENTO
Il Meeting dei Grandi Delegati al mio ufficio nel Febbraio 1926.

—

Dalle dimissioni, sino al comunicato del F. U. M. alla stampa, in Marzo 1926, rimasi muto e misterioso come una sfinge. Ero così nauseato, che bastava parlarmi dell'Ordine per cagionarmi un rivolgimento dello stomaco. Rifiutai quindi di ricevere un Comitato del Gran Concilio, che voleva esortarmi a ritirare le dimissioni.

Parecchie settimane dopo che la mente si era calmata, io ero tornato capace a giudicare l'Ordine spassionatamente con la fredda ragione del filosofo. Capparelli editore del "Nuovo Vessillo" insistette perchè io ricevessi un Comitato.

Prima erano venuti nel mio ufficio Mr. Lorrello e Mr. Sidoti ai quali esposi per oltre un ora la ragione delle dimissioni. Un altro giorno era stato da me Mr. Jannone, del Gran Concilio, a pregarmi di ritirare le dimissioni. Gli dissi che non potevo, in poche parole, giacchè egli sapeva l'affare del prestito e dell'inframmittenza di Miele negli affari del F. U. M.

Il Comitato di 15 Delegati, con Capparelli alla testa, venne nel mio ufficio, e vi rimase dalle 5 alle 9. Parlai a quei signori per tre ore. Volli giustificare a me stesso ed ai membri dell'Ordine che rispetto, il mio atto. Era dover mio esporre i fatti a loro, come era loro dovere, trovato che i fatti erano veri, produrre in seno all'Ordine un salutare rivolgimento.

Parlai, specialmente a quei signori dell'opera deleteria di Stefano Miele, lo spirito malefico dell'Ordine. Dissi ciò che costui avea tentato per vincermi, e compromettermi, coinvolgendo i membri del Gran Concilio, i quali erano o ciechi strumenti nelle mani di costui, o non capivano il pieno significato di ciò che facevano.

Spiegai la portata delle operazioni che Miele voleva; dissi delle sue insistenze per cacciar le mani nel F. M., ripetute in qualunque luogo, opportuno ed inopportuno, dinanzi alla Commissione e fuori, nel Gran Concilio o senza il Gran Concilio; dissi come ciò era rovinoso sotto ogni aspetto. Il gruppo di Schenectady era per domandare conto alla Sons of Italy Gran Lodge proprio del Fondo Mortuario. Con che faccia si sarebbe andati in Corte a reclamare il rendiconto di un fondo, che noi dalla nostra parte avevamo manomesso? In una "Court of equity" l'attore deve presentarsi con le mani perfettamente pulite. Se le ha sporche, non importa quanto sozze sieno quelle dell'avversario una "Court of Equity" non prenderà mai in considerazioni i piati d'un simile attore.

E supposto pure che la Sons of Italy Gran Lodge non si avvalesse d'una condizione cosi vantaggiosa, quell'atto potrebbe essere in qualunque tempo, da qualunque membro dell'Ordine rinfacciato a noi come una vergogna.

Io, dissi a quei delegati, ho impedito la cosa per oltre un mese e mezzo. Avrei potuto tenerla sospesa più a lungo, ma poi, vista la corrente dell'opinione contraria al mio giudizio, lasciai che la maggioranza decidesse ed assumesse la responsabilità dinanzi all'Ordine. Io pensavo non all'oggi, non al domani, ma al dopodomani, all'anno venturo, a quelli che seguiranno, quando gli ufficiali di oggi possono essere chiamati a rendere conto dei loro atti, compiuti in spregio alla moralità ed alla decenza della vita. Ma essi erano come una locomotiva che, senza il macchinista, precipita sconquassandosi e rumoreggiando, nell'abisso.

Dissi inoltre, essere impossibile far nulla nel Fondo Mortuario, mentre Miele era attorno. Egli ostruisce l'opera della Commissione in ogni modo, con proposte inacettabili ed insistenti malgrado l'irritazione che causavano.

Dissi come fossi ricorso al Grande Venerabile, perchè mi liberasse da quell'uomo ovvero sarei andato via io. Il Grande Venerabile fu del parere che egli non dovesse intervenire alle sedute della Commissione.

Ma ciò che volli che quei delegati intendessero bene, è il fatto che quanto accadde nel meeting del 12 Gennaio non fu la causa che determinò la risoluzione di dimettermi. Io ero circondato da ostacoli. Vedevo l'impossibilità di effettuare le più elementari cose appartenenti all'amministrazione dell'Ordine. Non potevo sopportare il costante, eterno, inafferrabile odio, nel quale avrei dovuto compiere la mia opera. Era un atmosfera ed un ambiente di disordinato, profondo e velenoso rancore verso gli individui. Mai una discussione intorno a idee, intorno agli ideali dell'Ordine, o degli Italiani in questo paese. Non era questione d'altro, lì dentro, che del come distruggere questo o quell'uomo. Era un atmosfera così pesante e grassa, premente su gli individui dell'Ordine, specialmnte quelli più in alto, che o una persona è presa da quello stesso odio contro individui, o si ribella e perde ogni influenza.

Dissi a quei signori che lo stesso Miele era il dominatore non solo nello Stato di New York ma anche nella Convenzione di Washington. Un influenza tanto più perniciosa e degradante in quanto, senza carica nella Gran Loggia, pure operava pesantemente ed invariabilmente.

Ora, il legato che avrei lasciato all'Ordine era l'esposizione dei fatti che mi avevano messo fuori. Un eredità preziosa abbastanza se i Grandi Venerabili volessero farne uso. Ma essi devono conoscere i fatti tenuti nascosti anche a loro.

Miele domina incontrastato. Volli studiare la psicologia dei membri della Commissione; ebbene, nominati tutti da Miele, non aveano la forza di opporsi alla sua volontà. Così i delegati dell'Up-State.

L'OSPEDALE ITALIANO

Un giorno Panetta venne da me, recando un giornale italiano, dove era annunziata un adunanza del Consiglio amministrativo dell'Ospedale Italiano. Era eccitatissimo perchè quegli altri, i Sons of Italy, tentavano di avere il dominio dell'Ospedale Italiano. La "gang" continuò a discutere su questo per interi giorni, finchè non venne dinanzi alla Commissione a domandare $200 per entrare in lista. Pagando il Gran Concilio $100 e $100 il Fondo mortuario acquistavano il diritto di essere rappresentati nel Consiglio dell'Ospedale.

L'Ordine dev'essere trascinato in tutte le lotte. L'Ordine non può essere lasciato tranquillo, e dovunque si rivelava qualche lotta da parte del gruppo oppositore, anche fuori gli Ambienti dell'Ordine, bisognava sopprimerla o controbilanciarla con una attività del nostro gruppo. Il cerchio si amplificò in tal modo, da includere quasi l'universo.

Io volli constatare se il corpo nazionale fosse così cancrenoso, come quello statale.

Andai a Washington è trovai che l'infezione nell'Organizzazione Nazionale era uguale a quella dello Stato. Vi predominano le stesse persone e prevalgono gli stessi metodi.

Il gruppo dominante voleva prelevare $2,500 e $1,700 dal Fondo Mortuario, ma rifiutava pagare le necessarie spese di amministrazione ed un adeguato salario agli impiegati, i quali erano mal pagati per quanto sovraccarichi di lavoro.

L'ipocrisia predominante dei leaders più attivi ed influenti mi nauseava.

Al meeting della crisi, del 12 Gennaio 1926 della Commissione, Stefano Miele e suo fratello si comportarono come facchini da strada, ruffiani e mascalzoni.

CAPITOLI V VI e VII.

LUSSI ESTIVI — ELENCO DELLE SPESE

Qui son riportati i totali di ciascun capitolo di spesa. Le partite, in dettaglio, possono leggersi nella parte inglese.

1. — Spese e pagamenti eseguiti per l'Ordine da Roberto Ferrari $608.95
2. — Stenografa e dattilografa per la Causa contro i Sons of Italy 154.00
3. — 3. Articoli inseriti nel Nuovo Vessillo. Pagato a Capparelli per cinque articoli 72.50
4. — Stenografa e dattilografa pei detti articoli 20.45

Oltre al compenso per il lavoro professionale di più mesi.

IL GUIDERDONE DEL LAVORO

Il prestito

Insieme alle pubblicazioni nei giornali, si ordina contro Ferrari una campagna di miserabili pettegolezzi, di dicerie intorno a prestiti ed a cambiali, con l'intento di divergere l'attenzione pubblica dall'Ordine e dai suoi travagli morali, per concentrarle sulle circostanze personali di chi quei travagli era stato costretto a rivelare.

Il 24 Aprile 1926 il Nuovo Vessillo pubblicò il riassunto di un discorso pronunziato da Miele con dei commenti di Capparelli editore del giornale.

Ecco ciò che il "Nuovo Vessillo", riportando il discorso di Miele, scrisse a pagina 3.

"La verità è che Roberto Ferrari avea bisogno di danaro e cominciò col fare domandare a me 500 dollari, proprio come ad un altro amico e fratello avea domandato 1000 dollari. Come fece altre volte rivolgendosi al Fratello Panetta e Panetta si rivolse a mio Fratello Umberto, che disse essere pronto a indorsare una cambiale firmata dall'avvocato Ferrari, ma Ferrari avea bisogno urgente e voleva il danaro senza molte cerimonie. Questa è la vera ragione del suo atteggiamento e della sua decisione."

Anche se questa storia fosse vera, la bassezza dell'individuo che la divulgò è sufficientemente dimostrata dalla stessa storia, e dalla condotta dell'editore del giornale, che dopo esser venuto al mio ufficio, per pregarmi, in presenza di 15 delegati, e piangendo in ginocchio, di ritirare le dimissioni e tornare nell'Ordine; dopo avermi innalzato ai sette cieli, nei suoi articoli adulatori, crede alle parole d'un bestione e non solo le pubblica, ma le condisce di commenti, sostenendole così:

"Roberto Ferrari, — scrive Capparelli — non sapendo, non potendo o non volendo combattere da uomo di coraggio, di fede e di onore, si ritirò in un modo eroi-comico dall'arena di combattimento.... ripudiando così non solo i suoi amici, ma anche l'istituzione di cui volea essere il nuovo apostolo ed il nuovo Messia. Diamo in questa pagina i punti più rilevanti del discorso del cavaliere Miele, che fu ascoltato con grande interesse".

Sono riportati nella parte inglese periodi di articoli stampati nel "Nuovo Vessillo" in Dicembre 1925 ed in Ottobre 1925 in cui ogni parola è una sperticata lode di Roberto Ferrari.

La verità della cosa può essere detta in poche parole.

Posso provare ogni parola, anche in questi futili incidenti personali, come ho potuto fare di ogni mia affermazione a riguardo dell'Ordine e della condotta di chi lo dirige.

Essi non possono provare nulla, perchè mentiscono, e colti all'improvviso, non ebbero tempo di foggiare falsi documenti.

Lavorai, come dissi in altra parte di questo Pamphlet, circa tre mesi, Agosto, Settembre ed Ottobre, quasi ogni ora del giorno e della notte per la causa contro i Sons of Italy Grand Lodge.

Ciò richiese non solo un enorme lavoro, ma un enorme impiego di energia e di danaro.

Il mio ufficio fu dedicato esclusivamente ai Figli d'Italia. Non potei, durante quel tempo, accettare nuove cause, nè attendere ad alcune in corso.

Il lavoro pei Figli d'Italia non solo era lungo, ma elaborato e complesso, e si compieva, per dippiù, sotto la più alta pressione.

Ciò che feci per l'Ordine, come avvocato, se avesso dovuto presentare il bill non sarebbe costato meno di $10.000.

Le mie spese personali intanto non venivano coperte da introiti. Aspettavo di incassare parecchi crediti. Avevo molti clienti che mi eran debitori per servizi professionali, ma oltre che io son di quelli cui non piace pressare, non avevo allora tempo di farlo.

Quando il Grande Venerabile, all'inizio della causa, in Agosto, disse che avevo diritto ad un anticipo, accettai l'offerta, che è consuetudinaria presso gli avvocati, ma, che dai Figli d'Italia non venne mai realizzata.

Nel Novembre gli avvocati americani insistettero per l'anticipo di $25.000, o avrebbero abbandonato la causa. La ditta desiderava conoscere quale parte avrebbero pretesa gli avvocati membri dell'Ordine.

Fu tenuta un adunanza di questi avvocati, facenti parte del Comitato Legale dell'Ordine, nell'ufficio del Grande Venerabile Freschi, dove la questione del nostro compenso fu discussa e decisa. Miele voleva il suo conpenso — non si sa perchè. Non avea certo funzionato da avvocato o procuratore, in quanto che, ignorando la legge, non capiva neppure di che noi discutevamo nel campo dei principi legali e della procedura. Probabilmente voleva esser pagato per avere fornito i dati di fatto su cui basava la causa. Il suo atteggiamento avrebbe disgustato chiunque.

Il Grande Venerabile si rivolse a me ed io risposi che avrei dato la mia decisione subito: non desideravo onorario di sorta pel mio lavoro passato ed avvenire. Ciò ebbe luogo in Dicembre, quando le mie condizioni finanziarie erano migliorate.

Disgraziatamente, nell'Ottobre ebbi bisogno di un piccolo aiuto finanziario e ricorsi a Panetta col quale ci scambiavamo dei favori. Egli conosceva quel che avevo fatto per l'Ordine, e come me prestava i suoi servigi gratuitamente. Promise di procurarmi un prestito di 500 dollari. A chi si rivolse a tutta prima non seppi, ma due settimane dopo fui informato che si era indirizzato ad Umberto Miele, il quale avea rifiutato recisamente sia di fare il prestito in contanti, sia di porre la firma su una cambiale. Panetta può attestare l'orrore che mi invase quando mi disse ciò. Avevo scampato un bel pericolo, quello di esser caduto in potere dei Miele, che mi avrebbero rinfacciato il prestito ad ogni controversia avessi avuto con loro.

Le mie relazioni con Miele, durante il periodo di associazione coi Figli d'Italia, furono le più fredde e formali. Sin dal principio ci sentivamo ostili e repulsivi l'uno all'altro. Entrambi avvertivamo di non appartenere alla stessa categoria umana.

Egli esibiva la sua persona dapertutto, in tutte le ovazioni. Fu lui che fece alterare i verbali, come imponeva la sua volontà alla Gran Loggia ed alla Suprema Convenzione. Lui e la sua "gang" vollero trascinar l'Ordine nei dissidi nelle risse nelle lotte e nello scisma.

Per riassumere la situazione. I metodi di questo Stefano Miele sono i metodi di oppressione e di prepotenza, della camorra e della mafia.

Nel discorso di Miele pubblicato dal "Vessillo" è detto che io domandai 1000 dollari ad un altro.

Questo è un affare ancor più semplice. Si, per semplice impulso di generosità non io domandai 1000 dollari, ma io detti in prestito 1000 dollari a Panetta, che in quei giorni pativa la fame, e bussava alle porte del F. U. M., per essere compensato dei suoi servigi.

Quest'uomo mostrò il mio check a Stefano Miele. Quando, molto tempo dopo, venni a saperlo e gli domandai perchè avea fatto ciò, rispose "volevo dimostrare quanto tu fossi solido e che carattere avessi. Panetta in quel tempo mi esaltava ovunque e sempre come un superuomo. Ho qui la copia fotografica del check.

* * *

Panetta ora è caduto così basso — un'altra vittima dell'Ordine — da divulgare il fatto intimo, privato che lui e suo fratello mi prestarono del danaro.

Quanto abbia a che fare tutto questo con la discussione intorno all'Ordine, non so vedere, nè alcuno saprebbe vedere eccetto persone dalla mente depravata ed irragionevole come Panetta e Miele.

Sissignore è vero. Panetta mi prestò, prima dell'Agosto 1925 $200.

Suo fratello, dopo l'Agosto mi prestò $200.

Ma è pure sacrosantamente vero che il 12 Novembre 1925 io detti a Panetta il check sopra fotografato di 1395 dollari. E cioè in restituzione dei $395 che ancora dovevo.

Più un grazioso prestito a lui di $1000.

I $200 dollari che Panetta mi prestò hanno una storia che merita d'essere accennata. Egli mi raccomandò un cliente in una causa penale. Il lavoro che feci meritava almeno $1000, ma per la sua raccomandazione, dissi mi sarei contentato di $600. Il cliente dichiarò che non potea pagare più di $100. Dissi a Panetta quanto tempo avevo speso e la natura del lavoro che avevo fatto. Panetta supplì alla deficienza del suo amico dandomi i 200 dollari, che io restituì.

Panetta, che narrò del prestito, tacque tutto ciò. Come non disse dei miei fraterni aiuti in ogni occasione, e come quando egli, dopo il meeting del 15 Gennaio del Gran Concilio con la Commissione del F. U. M., si trovò in gravi difficoltà per avere mutilato il resoconto dei verbali, con la soppressione della raccomandazione del Gran Concilio di aderire al prestito di $2.500, convocai un altro meeting del F. U. M. perchè si pronunziasse sul prestito.

Quest'uomo ora si avvoltola nelle bassezze della sua condotta fangosa. Mi dicono che racconti del suo prestito a me con chiunque si incontra. Son davvero fortunato se tutto ciò che possono dire contro di me si riduce a questo.

L'Interrogatorio

A questo punto è rivolto ai personaggi della Commedia un interrogatorio torturante e terribile cui quei signori non risponderanno ma potrà rispondere il pubblico, dopo aver letto attentamente la storia narrata in questo Pamphlet.

Tradurremo gli interrogativi che più significano e scottano.

F. Panetta — Questioni private

4. — E' da gentiluomo, se avete prestato danaro a qualcuno, raccontarlo ad una terza persona?

8. — Non è vero che voi qualificaste tutti i Miele "uova marcie e putrefatte?

15. — Non è vero che l'Ordine dei Figli d'Italia ricusava darvi alcun danaro, e voi eravate in terribili condizioni finanziarie e soffrivate la fame?

16. — Non è vero che domandaste denaro all'Ordine in compenso dei vostri servigi e nulla vi era stato dato sino al giorno 12 novembre?

18. — E' vero, o non è vero che voi odiate i Miele, ma rimanete dalla loro parte perchè nutrite un odio più grande per Cotillo?

21. — Diceste a persone estranee (cui raccontaste del prestito) dopo la rottura fra noi, che cosa feci per voi, finanziariamente, intellettualmente, moralmente e spiritualmente?

Domande a Freschi

4. — Non è vero che Miele richiese un compenso per la sua opera di avvocato della Grande Loggia?

14. — La sera del 15 Gennaio 1926, prima dell'adunanza del Gran Concilio e del F, U. M. non è vero che, chiamati in disparte voi Angrisani e Panetta narrai quanto era avvenuto nell'adunanza del 12 Gennaio in cui Miele e suo fratello Pasquale avevano verso di me pronunziate parole insultanti tentando di colpirmi?

15. — Non vi dissi che Stefano Miele avea dichiarato quanto segue:

1. — Se nell'Ordine non avessimo commesse illegalità e cose immorali non avremmo mai concluso nulla.

2. — Voi (riferendo a me) non conoscete la legge.

3. — Se un Giudice della Corte Suprema può fare cose illegali, ed immorali, lo potete (riferendo a me) anche voi.

4. — Voi (riferendosi a me) vi credete intelligente. Ve ne accorgerete. Vi aggiusterò io.

16. — Non vi indicai il tono con cui disse queste parole, specialmente le ultime, che egli mi avrebbe aggiustato per la mia opposizione al prestito?

18. — Non diceste che le azioni di Miele erano oltraggiose e che gli avreste parlato immediatamente, per eliminarlo dalla Commissione?

20. — Non vi dissi pure ciò che suo fratello Pasquale aveva detto e fatto?

29. — Non vi scrissi io, due o tre giorni prima della Convenzione di Washington dicendovi che ero ansioso di dare le dimissioni, adducendo alcune delle ragioni?

Domande ad Angrisani
(membro del Gran Concilio)

Sono sei e si riferiscono all'incidente dei Miele, alle dichiarazioni cioè di Stefano sull'opportunità delle cose immorali ed illegali, e sul linguaggio e gli atti camorristici di Pasquale.

Domande a M. De Pasquale

Sono ventisei. Riguardano le rimostranze che Ferrari fece a De Pasquale, segretario della Commissione del F. M., per l'ascendenza di Miele che subiva, per i verbali alterati che redigeva dietro pressioni del Miele, e per le comunicazioni che mandava alla stampa senza consultare Ferrari il Presidente.

Domande a Stefano Miele

Sono ventiquattro. Riguardano la domanda di prestito, la 4.a dice. Eravate voi autorizzato, (a fare la domanda) dal Gran Concilio?

6. — Se voi veniste autorizzato da una deliberazione mostrate la deliberazione registrata nei verbali del Gran Concilio.

7. — Compariste dinanzi alla Commissione del Fondo Mortuario nuovamente il 12 Gennaio per ottenere il prestito di $2.500?

8. — Nella stessa sera veniste a domandare un prestito addizionale di $1.700 per pagare le spese dei grandi delegati?

12. — Non è vero che volevate un compenso pel vostro lavoro d'avvocato nella causa dell'Ordine Figli d'Italia contro la Sons of Italy Grand Lodge?

13. — Quanto chiedeste?

17. — Non è vero che sopprimeste parte delle mie lettere inviate alle Logge subordinate, quando vi arrogaste l'autorità di leggere le lettere nei meetings?

19. — Non è vero che vostro fratello durante il meeting del F. U. M. del 12 Gennaio mi rivolse parole insultanti?

20. — Non è vero che mi venne vicino e levò il braccio, tentando di colpirmi?

22. — Non diceste a De Pasquale di non mettere nei verbali che eravate apparso dinanzi alla Commissione il 12 Gennaio 1926 per domandare un prestito di $2.500 per gli avvocati ed un altro di $1.700 pei Grandi Delegati che dovevano recarsi alla Convenzione di Washington?

23. — Non è vero che, ad un meeting di avvocati e non avvocati, nell'ufficio degli avvocati americani, rivolto a Roberto Ferrari, in presenza dei membri del Comitato presenti, diceste: "Noi avremo Ferrari per interrogare Cotillo?"

24. — Non è vero che Ferrari rispose immediatamente "Ferrari non interrogherà Cotillo"?

Domande ai Membri del Fondo Mortuario

I 5 interrogativi rivolti ai componenti la Commissione del F. U. M. tendono a stabilire che Stefano Miele chiese il prestito senza l'autorizzazione del Grande Concilio, che nel meeting del 12 Gennaio pronunziò le note parole in spregio della legalità e della moralità, nonchè le parole oltraggiose e gli atti camorristici di Pasquale Miele.

Sulle identiche posizioni si aggirano le sei domande indirizzate ad Aliprandi, uno della Commissione del F. U. M.

Domande a Frank Panetta

Sono quarantaquattro. Traduciamo le principali.

1. — Non è vero che odiate Cotillo al punto che fareste e direste qualunque cosa, non importa quanto rovinosa pel carattere di chicchessia, pur di tenere insieme il gruppo dell'Ordine Figli d'Italia allo scopo di distruggere, per mezzo di esso, Cotillo?

2. — Prima delle Convenzioni di New York e di Schenectady, non mi cercaste per indurmi ad andare ai meetings, all'Hotel Pennsylvania, del gruppo Miele Freschi, che preparava un piano d'azione?

6. — Ho io mai assistito ad un meeting di questo gruppo all'Hotel Pennsylvania, o altrove?

7. — Non è vero che volevate io agissi da Speciale Grande Oratore per processare i Membri del Gran Consiglio dello Stato di New York, i quali erano allora accusati dinanzi al Supremo Comitato arbitrale?

8. — Volli io accettare ed agire da grande oratore?

15. — Non vi parlai dell'importanza della deliberazione nella questione dei prestiti di 2500 e di 1700 dollari e non vi dissi che essi tentavano di rovinarmi e persistevano nei loro sforzi?

16. — Non vi dissi che volevo uscire dai pasticci al più presto possibile?

39. — In Agosto, Settembre e Ottobre non aveste a litigare, molte volte, cogli impiegati dell'ufficio, e minacciare di allontanarvi?

40. — Non volevate voi cose che la famiglia dei Miele vi negò, e malgrado ciò voi rimaneste tra loro?

44. — E' vero che ora, mentre il vostro gruppo è sottosopra, per le dimissioni di Ferrari, intendete, a causa dell'odio contro Cotillo ed

il desiderio di vincere a qualunque costo, malignare contro Ferrari e cercare di macchiarne la reputazione, fino al punto di mentire anche intorno alle cose sue private che non hanno nulla a che vedere con gli affari dell'Ordine?

Gli americani devono sapere le condizioni dell'Ordine Figli d'I-talia, e come le persone che lo sgovernano son ben lungi dall'essere i suoi veri rappresentanti.

Se la situazione non viene presentata chiaramente e definitiva-mente al pubblico americano questo non avrà mai un idea corretta dell'elevazione e della distinzione degli Italiani in America.

Cattivi rappresentanti delle razze, in questo paese, hanno enorme-mente danneggiato quella razza!

Avvertiamo gli americani che questa gente, che spadroneggia, non è se non la schiuma venuta a galla, ma non rappresenta la parte sostanziale degli italiani in America.

La luce della pubblicità, la discussione intorno all'Ordine sperde-ranno la materia combustibile, che maltratta e deforma l'Ordine al cospetto del pubblico americano.

Gli Italiani hanno bisogno dell'aiuto del pubblico americano per estrarre dal seno dell'Ordine il cancro che ne corrode il cuore.

CAPITOLO VIII.

IO ACCUSO

—

Li accuso di trascurare i principi.

Li accuso di trascurare le idee.

Li accuso di mancanza di ideali.

Li accuso di negligere onorevoli occasioni a favore degli Italiani nello Stato di New York.

Li accuso di odiare profondamente e lungamente le persone.

Li accuso della più alta ipocrisia.

Li accuso di alterare i verbali.

Li accuso di aver reso impossibile di avere nei verbali un riflesso esatto di quanto era accaduto nelle adunanze.

Li accuso di brutalità verbale e fisica.

Li accuso di impedire la libera discussione.

Li accuso di avarizia e grettezza verso gli impiegati e di selvagge stravaganze coi fondi per cose non appartenenti al Fondo Mortuario.

Li accuso di aver tentato di fare di me una figura decorativa.

Li accuso di aver resistito ai miei sforzi per liberarmi dagli ostacoli di gente estranea e dalle loro catene, eccetto le catene della legge e della moralità.

Li accuso di avere usato meco dapprima blandizie a carezze, per indurmi ai loro desiderii.

Li accuso, quando le blandizie e le carezze fallirono, di avere usato coercizione mentale e forza fisica.

Li accuso di aver messo a carico del Fondo Mortuario spese che la commissione non avea autorizzata.

Li accuso di aver tentato far di me lo strumento ed il complice di una "gang" di saccheggiatori, che domina l'Ordine.

Accuso Stefano Miele di presunzione, ampollosità e stupidaggine.

Lo accuso di odiare velenosamente molte persone e i Sons of Italy Grand Lodge.

Lo accuso di violare le leggi.

Lo accuso di pratiche tenebrose nella commissione e fuori.

Lo accuso di abusare della posizione strategica che ha nell'Ordine per intimorire ed imporre la sua volontà sui deboli ed impotenti Commissari e membri del Gran Concilio.

Lo accuso di tiranneggiare i Membri della Commissione e del Gran Concilio.

Lo accuso di aver presentato proposte illegali alla Commissione ed al Gran Concilio.

Lo accuso di avere indotti ed istigati questi membri a violare, non solo le leggi dell'Ordine, ma la legge generale dello Stato di New York, la legge morale e la legge comune di decente comportamento nella società umana.

Lo accuso di avere impedito qualsiasi amichevole aggiustamento del caso contro la Sons of Italy Grand Lodge, con la sua tattica scellerata ed ostruzionista, dopo che il Comitato di avvocati per l'attore aveva discusso un accordo amichevole, almeno durante la pendenza della lite.

Lo accuso di avere influenzato il Grande Venerabile a non accettare l'accordo per speciose, insostenibili ed egoistiche ragioni.

Lo accuso di risentire profondamente e di nutrire odio contro molti individui della Sons of Italy Grand Lodge e particolarmente contro il Giudice della Suprema Corte Salvatore Cotillo.

Lo accuso di aver tentato di trascinarmi in questo cerchio di veleno e di odio per suoi scopi.

Lo accuso di aver tentato di avvalersi di me per interrogare il giudice Cotillo, tentativo che produsse in me un immediata reazione, che Miele non dimenticherà mai.

Lo accuso della più svergognata sfacciataggine.

Lo accuso di bassezza che gli fa usare nella lotta le armi più vili.

Lo accuso di avere ricorso alla sola difesa che egli sia capace di concepire, una difesa che, anche se vera, non sarebbe stata usata da nessun uomo d'onore.

Accuso il clan dei Miele d'essersi messi in posizioni strategiche nell'Ordine, nel Supremo Concilio, nel Fondo Mortuario e nel Gran Concilio allo scopo di controllare e dominare in ogni sfera di azione l'Ordine dei Figli d'Italia.

CAPITOLO IX.

LUCE ED OMBRA

Non rimpiango quel che mi accadde e le perdite di tempo e di danaro.

La conoscenza che feci in 6 mesi di uomini e cose nei Figli d'Italia mi varrà per combattere il resto della mia vita.

Gli Italiani in questo paese hanno un grande avvenire. Questo non deve esser messo in pericolo dagli uomini che, al presente, infestano l'Ordine dei Figli d'Italia. I riflessi che la vita italiana getta sulla scena americana son carichi di ombre profonde.

L'Ordine dev'essere purificato, non solo per sè stesso, ma per eliminare gli ostacoli che sono sulla via degli Italiani. Coi politicanti nell'Ordine dei Figli d'Italia, che vogliono usarlo per avanzare ed ingrandirsi, e che complottano assiduamente con i politicanti e gli uomini pubblici americani per cavare le castagne dal fuoco, l'Ordine è certo su falsa strada.

E' sulla via d'una rapida distruzione. La distruzione dell'Ordine si ripercuoterà sugli italiani d'America. Ma la ripercussione sarà di breve durata.

Il meglio, che potrebbe accadere agli Italiani negli Stati Uniti, a meno che non avvenga uno spazzamento generale degli uomini delle pratiche e dei metodi in voga, è la sparizione dalla vita italiana di un Ordine che solo degrada gli italiani agli occhi degli Americani.

Un Ordine, come quello esistente ritarda o impedisce l'americanizzazione che noi speriamo ed ardentemente ci auguriamo. Gli Italiani devono divenire parte e particella del pubblico americano. Essi non potranno diventare carne ed ossa del corpo politico americano, se non si liberano dai falsi profeti che li sviarono, e non abbandonano i metodi tenebrosi finora seguiti.

Gli Italiani dovrebbero vergognarsi di loro stessi. Sono oltre tre milioni negli Stati Uniti, e quasi un milione nella città di New York, ed è oltremodo difficile che di buon accordo ed in armonia essi compiano qualcosa di nobile e di utile.

Tante istituzioni, tante cose sarebbero necessarie per gli italiani, ma nulla si crea. Vi è troppa ansia di emergere nei singoli individui, e troppo personalismo. Non esiste quello spirito di fusione individuale nel bene comune, che esiste presso altre razze negli Stati Uniti. Gli Ebrei hanno iniziata proprio ora, una campagna per raccogliere quindici milioni di dollari, sei dei quali devono raccogliersi nella Città di New York.

Che cosa non potrebbero fare gli Italiani se potessero mettere assieme $1.000.000? Ma se anche riuscissero a raccogliere un milione, accadrebbero tanta contese fra i dirigenti ed i leaders, che l'armonia dell'azione sarebbe paralizzata e nulla si concluderebbe, anche col danaro.

La cosa più importante per gli Italiani è frantumare i leaders che li tradirono, cominciare la vita di nuovo con altri uomini, e mutare questa loro psicologia di inazione e di sospetto con una attività e fiducia insieme a persone che di fiducia son meritevoli.

Segue la confutazione minuta e precisa di tutte le affermazioni contenute nei comunicati ufficiali del Marzo 29 dell'Aprile 26 nonchè della Circolare N. 21.

Le confutazioni si basano su otto lettere autentiche, riportate testualmente, sui verbali, su testimonianze e su argomenti logici inconfutabili. . . . .

E' così dimostrata la inaccuratezza e falsificazione dei verbali; il perchè le dimissioni furono date con poche parole, senza rassegnare le ragioni; l'insulsaggine dell'accusa che Ferrari tentò sollevare odi; le ragioni perchè venne firmato il check; l'accusa assurda che Ferrari intendesse suscitare una rivoluzione nelle file dell'Ordine.

* * *

Anche l'articolo pubblicato in tre numeri del "Nuovo Mondo" 4, 6 e 7 Maggio 1926 non è che la confutazione anzi la distruzione del comunicato del Fondo unico Mortuario, col quale si intendeva rispondere a quanto io affermai nel mio comunicato e narrai ad Ernesto Valentini in un intervista apparsa pure nel "Nuovo Mondo" e che qui sotto e ristampata insieme con gli articoli pubblicati in Zarathustra.

ROBERTO FERRARI NON FA PIU' PARTE DELL'ORDINE FIGLI D'ITALIA

(Dalla Rivista Zarathustra di Marzo 1926)

E' accaduto quel che prevedevamo.

Dopo soli nove mesi di contatto con i Grandi, i Supremi Venerabili, gli Oratori i Segretari, i Concilii, i fondi mortuari o educativi Roberto Ferrari è uscito nauseato dall'Ordine.

I lettori ci intendano bene. Le molte migliaia di lavoratori e piccoli borghesi italiani aggregati all'Ordine da essi alimentato con le contribuzioni mensili, meritano simpatia ed interesse tanto maggiori quanto più sono sfruttati e turlupinati da una cricca di faccendieri che predominano e spadroneggiano.

Ma, nelle condizioni attuali, l'Ordine non può sollevarsi di un pollice al di sopra delle cafoniche e vecchie società di mutuo soccorso, da cui — come ha lucidamente dimostrato Baldo Aquilano — esso deriva. Il marcio è in taluni dirigenti, non nella sana massa del popolo. L'Ordine, però, oggi deprime.

Dacchè Fiorello La Guardia si tuffò sino ai capelli nelle acque melmose di esso, ha livellato la sua statura politica e sociale, che appariva così promettente di sviluppo, alla sua statura fisica.

Che in esso, date le attuali condizioni, non possano trovare ambiente adeguato caratteri onesti e menti superiori, è provato dal caso di Roberto Ferrari.

Questi entrò nell'organizzazione nove mesi or sono quando l'Ordine era in pieno disordine.

Credette il male passeggero e rimediabile.

Andò a Schenectady perchè impressionato e convinto dell'illegalità dell'azione della Sons of Italy Grand Lodge e del famoso atto d'incorporazione. Ma al di fuori delle pure questioni legali, nulla sapeva o sospettava delle purulenze interne e nascoste nel sodalizio.

Se ne convinse dopo la recente convenzione di Washington, la quale, come accennammo nell'altro numero, fu un vero scandalo.

Erano colà 35 delegati, invece di 12, quanti doveano e potevano essere legalmente, dopo la secessione. Ogni mille Figli, infatti, sono rappresentati da un delegato. Dei 35 mila iscritti nello Stato di New York, soli 12 mila aderirono alla Convenzione di Schenectady. Furono creati a Washington gli altri 23 delegati?

La proroga dei poteri a Di Silvestro ebbe luogo a mezzo d'un ignobile colpo di mano.

La Convenzione fu condotta con sistemi così autocratici, che un delegato si levò per proporre, ironicamente, che "la prossima convenzione sia fatta per corrispondenza".

Disgustava il sistema antiparlamentare che impediva qualsiasi apparenza di discussione.

Ferrari, in quell'adunanza, sentì tutto il dissidio fra la sua educazione, la sua mente e l'ambiente che lo circondava.

Questo parve a lui così profondamente guasto ed insanabile, che non vide altra uscita che nelle dimissioni.

Si può rimanere in un'organizzazione quando le divergenze sono di idee e di programmi, non quando provengono dal carattere morale e dai mezzi adoperati per vivere giornalmente.

Per combattere le persone che di quei mezzi si servono bisognava usare armi e sistemi ripugnanti. Non valeva la spesa.

Egli vide il modo come si dispone e si usano i fondi raccolti dai poveri ingenui, che pagano, obbediscono ed ignorano.

Volevano che lui, presidente del fondo mortuario, intangibile al di fuori del suo scopo ben determinato, prelevasse il denaro da dare agli avvocati della ditta Hugues, che assunsero la difesa contro i Sons of Italy. Volevano che si prelevassero $1700 per i delegati grandi e piccoli, che dovevano recarsi a Washington.

Ferrari resistette. Io non tocco, disse, non abuso del denaro confidatomi pel fondo mortuario, non per i vostri viaggi ed i vostri avvocati. Aggiunse: Come potete domandare conto dei fondi alla grande Loggia dei "Sons of Italy" se voi commettete uguali manomissioni?

Ci fu chi rispose: ma queste cose si possono coprire. Come? Con artificiose menzogne? Coprire una porcheria non è distruggerla. Fu proposto alla Ditta Hugues il quesito della legalità del prelevamento osteggiato da Ferrari. La Ditta rispose: Se preleverete $1700 per le spese dei delegati a Washington, commetterete atto illegale; se preleverete $2500 per l'acconto da pagare alla Ditta Hughes il vostro atto è legalissimo e meritorio. Il responso fu umanamente grande, ma non convinse Ferrari. Egli aveva lavorato notte e giorno, tre mesi interi, per studiare ed istruire la causa contro i Sons of Italy, senza domandare nè ricevere un soldo.

Durante una viva discussione l'avvocato Stefano Miele accusò Ferrari di ignorare la legge, perciò il Fondo Unico Mortuario non doveva lasciarsi impressionare dalle sue parole.

Ferrari allora incalzò, dimostrando l'illegalità e la immoralità della manomissione con tale lucidezza che l'avvocato Miele, non sapendo più che rispondere scoppiò in una magnifica confessione: "Ma se, nell'Ordine, "disse, non si fossero fatte cose illegali ed immorali non si sarebbe concluso mai nulla! ! !" Poi soggiunse: "Se un giudice della Corte Suprema può far cose immorali ed illegali, puoi farle anche tu!"

Questa è la moralità? questi sono i maggiorenti dell'Ordine dei Figli d'Italia? Ferrari, più che mai determinato di staccarsi dal signor Miele si dimise.

Le condizioni scoperte da Ferrari nelle due Loggie dello Stato di New York, e nel così detto Concilio Supremo — a quanto dicono gli esperti — sono uguali in tutta la Nazione.

Ferrari era incompatibile con l'Istituzione italiana. Da questa lo separava un'alta aristocrazia morale ed intellettuale, nonchè una concezione opposta delle finalità della vita e dei mezzi per raggiungerla.

Mentre l'Ordine, da cui egli esce, mira al vantaggio materiale di un manipolo di sfruttatori furbi a danno della massa, vantaggi conseguiti col gesuitismo, l'ipocrisia, la menzogna e l'imbroglio, egli di mente fertile e larga mira a risultati di progresso sociale collettivo da conseguirsi con la forza dell'intelletto e l'integrità esemplare del carattere. Egli è un leader del pensiero, e troppo grande è la sproporzione fra l'angustia mentale dell'Ordine e le idealità di Ferrari, ben diverse dai piccoli vantaggi di cui vivono i condottieri dell'Ordine.

Persino nelle forme esteriori di comportamento e di linguaggio Ferrari avvertiva un'antitesi insopportabile. Ed infine manca a lui il fanatismo dell'italianità o dell'americanismo, che l'Ordine affetta maliziosamente, per trarre da esso miserabili piccoli profitti.

Quando Ferrari, insomma, vide che l'avvocato Stefano Miele sintetizza e riflette l'anima e la mente dell'Ordine dei Figli d'Italia che dirige di sottomano,, pensò: qui io non posso stare. Se ne andò, e fece bene.

LO SFACELO MORALE DELL'ORDINE FIGLI D'ITALIA

(Da Zarathustra di Aprile 1926)

Appare ora, in tutta la sua miseria.

Documenti e fatti sono dinanzi al pubblico, alla portata di chi vuol sapere e vedere la realtà.

Baldo Aquilano, nella Storia dell'Ordine dei Figli d'Italia, fissò l'origine di questo. Non è che un aggruppamento delle antiche "Società di Mutuo Soccorso, "tipo coloniche — scrive Aquilano — che non erano palestra di educazione, non insegnarono il mutuo amore, ma erano un esempio innegabile della nostra sterile, nauseante e disgustevole vita associativa coloniale ,inutile per sè e per gli altri, eterno campo di sfruttamento a danno suo ed a profitto degli altri."

Dalla storia di Aquilano si rileva, altresì, che i caratteri originali, continuarono, anzi si acuirono, durante i venti anni dacchè l'Ordine esiste.

Per impressionare la fantasia degli operai, e dei contadini ignoranti, delle antiche Società, si istituirono riti massonici misteriosi, sciarpe, placche, paludamenti sacerdotali, formule sacre, iniziazioni ridicolmente spettacolose ed infine il giuramento che attanaglia la debole coscienza del povero cafone, il quale si crede avvinto per esso ad un fato arcano misterioso e potente.

Che cosa potete sperare da un organizzazione di tal fatta, sorta in America in pieno secolo ventesimo, fra la crisi travolgente non del passato medioevale su cui è basato l'Ordine, ma delle ideologie morali, sociali ed economiche più moderne?

Così, quest'Ordine dei Figli d'Italia, visse venti anni, coltivando le sue discordie, le sue misere porcherie, i suoi Fondi Mortuari, la sua inutile burocrazia, nell'immenso nulla della sua gonfiatura, e fra l'indifferenza e la disattenzione generale.

Ma quando, sopravvenuto l'uragano fascista, si tentò farne uno strumento politico italiano, servile e reazionario, lo sguardo della comunità italiana qui emigrata cominciò a considerarlo e studiarlo. Prima, chi, al difuori dei segretari e degli oratori grandi si, ma poveramente retribuiti, si occupava dell'Ordine?

Sorta la questione fascista, ecco che i sovversivi, figlietti d'Italia, anch'essi pacifici e distratti sino allora, si rizzarono arditi e violenti contro chi mercanteggiava, a Roma, il gregge pecorile.

Fu l'azione politico fascista di Disilvestro che rese l'Ordine "up to date". Si fece rumore. Il rumore attira l'attenzione. L'attenzione fece scoprire le schermaglie politico personali di Cotillo e Disilvestro. Molti si schierarono dall'una o dall'altra parte. Venne lo scisma e tutto il resto.

Seguimmo la crisi anche noi. Accennammo alle lettere dei capi. A queste seguirono, specie nel "Nuovo Mondo", pubbliche denunzie ed attacchi di ascritti all'Ordine, che non vale la pena riportare, dopo avere riassunto il libro di Aquilano, perchè non sono che un esempio più largo ed attuale, dello spirito di dissidenza cainesca, che è la sola cosa vera e tangibile dell'Ordine.

Senonchè, scoppiata, da ultimo, la pubblica denunzia dei costumi etici e legali dell'Ordine, per parte dell'Avvocato Roberto Ferrari, tutto l'intimo sfacelo del sodalizio appare evidente e chiaro.

L'avvocato Ferrari — notisi — fu trascinato pei capelli a svelare fatti ed impressioni, che forse avrebbe tenuti nascosti, da quel disgraziato comunicato ufficiale con cui si volle dare una spiegazione qualsiasi al suo allontanamento.

Ora, per riparare alla disastrosa impressione della intervista, nonchè della risposta al comunicato ufficiale, si fanno correre assurde storielle di aspettative finanziarie deluse ed altrettante corbellerie, inventate di sana pianta.

Qui sotto è riportata, oltre l'intervista testuale di Roberto Ferrari, una lettera di G. B. d'Ausilio che dimostra in che conto è tenuto l'Ordine dei Figli d'Italia quando si arriva a supporre che da esso possano emanare aggressioni alle spalle, come in piena mala vita. Non crediamo alle aggressioni, ma rimaniamo profondamente impressionati da un insieme di cose che reclama l'aiuto e la cooperazione di quanti cittadini d'origine italiana sentono la solidarietà di razza ed il rispetto di sè stessi.

Non è da disperare della massa. Il popolo è capace di progresso. Bisogna averne cura, non per sfruttarlo, non per carpirgli qualche dollaro al mese, ma per aprirgli la mente ed ambientarlo all'epoca ed al paese.

Quelli che incancrenirono l'Associazione non sono che pochi. Quelli che potrebbero agire saggiamente ed intelligentemente sono moltissimi. Perchè rimangono in disparte? Perchè lasciano fare e malfare?

Sopratutto è necessario che i giovani italo-americani, più capaci e più attivi, si facciano innanzi a prendere in cura questi cento o centocinquantamila italiani che desidererebbero associarsi per affrontare poderosamente o almeno in condizioni meno svantaggiose degli altri i problemi dell'esistenza in America.

Le masse sono stupide, ma docili. Hanno bisogno di buoni condottieri.

L'Ordine dei Figli d'Italia — lo ripetiamo e lo ripeteremo ancora — se vuol essere ed essere qualcosa di rispettabile e di serio, deve disinfettarsi, deve riformarsi. Se no a lui spetta la fine, o peggio ancora, la continuazione della sua mala vita.

PERCHE' L'AVV. FERRARI SI STACCO' DAI FIGLI D'ITALIA

Intervista con Ernesto Valentini
dal "Nuovo Mondo"

Il comunicato alla stampa apparso nel "Corriere d'America", disse così:

"Il segretario del Fondo Unico Mortuario dell'Ordine Figli d'Italia in America ci comunica:

"Quale Segretario del Fondo Unico Mortuario, sono stato autorizzato a mandare alla stampa il seguente statement.

"Molte cose si sono dette intorno alle dimissioni dell'Avv. R. Ferrari da Presidente del F. U. M.

"Si è detto che le dimissioni dell'Avv. Ferrari furono provocate dal fatto che l'Avv. Stefano Miele voleva $3000 dal F. U. M. l'avv. Ferrari si dimise per ragioni sue particolari indipendenti dall'Amministrazione del F. U. M.

"L'Avv. Stefano Miele incaricato dal Grande Concilio, con regolare deliberazione, venne innanzi alla Commissione del F. U. M. per chiedere un prestito di $2500.00 pei bisogni urgenti ed improrogabili di quella Amministrazione. La Commissione avendo fondi sufficienti e disponibili accolse la proposta e l'Avv. Ferrari, quale presidente, firmò il check che consegnò nelle mani del Comm. J. Freschi il quale a sua

volta lo consegnò al grande segretario di finanza che fece la corrispon-
dente entrata nei registri contabili. Questa è la verità vera e chiunque
intenda constatare questa verità cinta di quercia, è cortesemente pregato favorire nei nostri uffici, in qualunque ora del giorno, ed anche
fuori le ore d'Ufficio, per leggere la deliberazione del prestito, osservare il check che è già di ritorno dalla banca e quanto altro possa occor-
rere o sarà necessario per calmare le menti sature di fantastiche e mastodontiche calunnie."

Il comunicato stampato nel "Progresso", comincia pure con le parole. "Molte cose si son dette intorno alle dimissioni dell'Avv. Ferrari"
e via di seguito, però, alla fine, le "menti" non sono come nel "Corriere" "sature di fantastiche e mastodontiche "dicerie". Inoltre contiene
una circostanza omessa nel comunicato del "Corriere". Questa: Pregato
l'Avv. Miele a smentire tali dicerie ha risposto: "ch'egli è troppo alto
nella propria e nell'altrui estimazione per sentirsi tocco da tante volga-
rità che rasentano la calunnia."

Evidentemente il segretario che formulò il Comunicato non ebbe
un'idea definita e chiara intorno alle "calunnie" denunziate, se, nel
"Corriere" sono mastodontiche" ma nel "Progresso" si mutano in "dicerie" e nell'altera auto esaltazione di Miele, si cangiano in "volgari-
tà, non mastodonticamente calunniose, ma appena "rasentanti la calunnia."

Ad ogni modo, pensai essere opportuno interrogare Roberto Ferrari pei lettori del "Nuovo Mondo" che si interessano al gran rumore
giornalistico dei "Figli d'Italia".

Chi meglio di lui, può dare la spiegazione dell'enigmatico Comunicato Ufficiale?

Qualche circostanza raccolta da me — dopo la pubblicazione del
Comunicato — per "Zarathustra", indicava inoltre l'opportunità di ap-
profondire una controversia, che sotto l'apparenza personale, contiene fatti rivelanti la vera essenza attuale dell'Ordine.

Andai, dunque, da Roberto Ferrari.

— Bada, gli dissi, che quanto sono per domandarti e quanto ri-
sponderai è per essere pubblicato nel "Nuovo Mondo"

Quali sono le "ragioni tue particolari, indipendenti dall'Amministrazione del Fondo Unico Mortuario" che ti indussero — come dice
il Comunicato Ufficiale — ad uscire dall'Ordine?

— "Nessuna ragione" particolare indipendente dall'Amministrazione del F. U. M. ma "molte ragioni" non particolari, e strettamente
dipendenti dal modo come si procede nell'Amministrazione del F. U.
M. nonchè in tutto l'Ordine.

— Specifica, se credi, queste ragioni.

— Innanzi tutto devo dire che il "Rank and File" ossia le masse
dell'Ordine dimostrarono verso di me la più grande fiducia; fiducia
che non potevo, nè dovevo disilludere. Iniziai, quindi, la mia opera
nell'Ordine con entusiasmo di alte idealità.

Ben presto, però, mi accorsi che l'azione dei dirigenti era infor-
mata a criterii e metodi, opposti a quelli che io avrei potuto adottare
o seguire. E poichè non potevo sperare di riuscire a modificare quei
metodi; nè era possibile adattarmi ad essi, vidi ben presto le origini di
un dissidio che avrebbe inevitabilmente prodotto il mio allontanamento.

— Puoi darmi qualche esempio di tali metodi?

— Molti esempi. Comincio dall'ultimo: il modo, cioè, come annunziarono, a mezzo della stampa, il mio ritiro.

Il comunicato non è veritiero, nè leale. Tende non ad informare il pubblico o i fratelli dell'Ordine, ma a proiettare su me un'ombra dubbia. Perchè dice: "ragioni sue particolari indipendenti dall'Amministrazione del F. U. M." senza specificare una, almeno, delle ragioni particolari? Te lo dico io il perchè. Perchè le "ragioni mie particolari indipendenti dall'Amministrazione del F. U. M." non esistono; e le ragioni non particolari ma generali, connesse con l'Amministrazione del F. U. M. essi non osano dirle.

— Perchè non osano?

— Perchè intendono amministrare, e di fatto amministrano i danari dell'Ordine, con criteri di libera disponibilità, che non sono conformi... agli statuti.

— Cita, se puoi, casi concreti.

— Non è difficile. Mi proposero e pretendevano che io consentissi a prelevare dal Fondo Unico Mortuario $2500 con cui pagare gli avvocati che sostenevano la causa contro la "Sons of Italy Grand Lodge", e $1700 per le spese dei delegati che dovevano recarsi alla Convenzione di Washington. Io sapevo bene che non si poteva, quindi non si doveva. Il F. U. M. è un "Trust Fund" vale a dire un fondo fiduciario da usarsi solo per le ragioni ed i fini per cui fu creato.

— Ma allora, perchè fecero stampare: "L'Avv. Ferrari quale Presidente firmò il check?"

— Siffatto modo di presentare le cose è uno dei loro metodi di mistificazione e d'inganno. I fatti sono questi. Miele venne nella Commissione del F. U. M. e propose di stornare dal Fondo $2500 per gli avvocati e più tardi voleva $1700 pei delegati. Non già, come si dice nel comunicato, "incaricato dal Grande Concilio con regolare deliberazione", il che non è vero, ma dopo verbali e privati accordi con altri ufficiali. In quell'adunanza Miele espose le ragioni del prelevamento. Io richiesi il parere dei commissari. Per lasciare ad essi piena libertà di pensiero e di parola non manifestai la mia opinione. Mi accorsi presto che erano tutti d'accordo per l'atto illegale. Esposi allora le ragioni che mi facevano opporre la proposta, ragioni ovvie ed intuitive, che non occorre ripetere.

Miele insistette. Per non precipitare una decisione feci presente che una deliberazione, quella sera, sarebbe stata illgale, per l'assenza dei commissari dell'Up-State, i quali non erano stati invitati.

I commissari presenti convennero e la questione fu rimandata.

Alla prossima adunanza Stefano Miele ripropose la stessa cosa.

Mi opposi energicamente, riuscendo anche quella sera, ad evitare una decisione. Speravo che col tempo ed una maggior riflessione si sarebbe scongiurato quell'errore.

Fu in quel meeting che Miele rivelò la mia "ignoranza della Legge". Infatti io allora ignoravo "la legge" ma non la legge dell'Ordine dei Figli d'Italia e del più comune senso morale, ma ignoravo la sua legge, che spiegò lucidamente nello stesso meeting con le seguenti parole: "Ma se non si fossero fatte nell'Ordine cose illegali ed immorali non si sarebbe mai concluso nulla"

Si ribadì allora nell'animo mio la prima impressione, che s'era sempre più rafforzata, del dissidio assoluto fra il mio criterio di condotta ed il loro.

Quella sera, ancora, riuscii ad evitare una decisione.

Il giorno dopo telefonai al Grande Venerabile per avvertirlo dell'inframmettenza di Miele nella Commissione che presiedevo, e per sapere se i Grandi Ufficiali approvavano o no il modo di agire di Miele.

Feci intendere che se questo non fosse stato eliminato dalla Commissione del F. U. M. io mi sarei immediatamente dimesso.

Miele fu allontanato e le dimissioni furono pel momento evitate.

Senonchè egli si dette con ardore ad influenzare, al di fuori delle adunanze, tanto i Commissari del F. U. M., quanto i grandi Ufficiali.

Così avvenne che quando ebbe luogo, per suggerimento del Grande Venerabile, un'adunanza del Grande Concilio e della Commissione del F. U. M. riuniti, mi accorsi che erano tutti d'accordo con lui.

— Perchè accettasti questa grande adunanza. Che cosa speravi?

— Volevo esporre al Gran Concilio i termini della controversia ed indagare quale era il loro pensiero intorno alla condotta di Miele. Durante la discussione si parlò di raccomandare alla Commissione di accettare lo storno. Dichiarai che anche con la raccomandazione mi sarei opposto. Ma, senti quello che accadde.

Dopo quel meeting, in cui l'eloquenza corse a fiumi, si tennero altre due adunanze della Commissione.

Nella prima richiesi il processo verbale del meeting riunito. Trovai che la raccomandazione di accettare il prelevamento non era stata notata.

— Come mai?

— Se ne dimenticarono! Ad ogni modo, sorpreso della dimenticanza, ma non scosso nelle mie convinzioni evitai, anche quella sera di porre ai voti il prelevamento. Nacque un pandemonio. Uno dei commissari insisteva si votasse. Riuscii nondimeno a rimandare ad una altra seduta.

Venne il meeting finale. Mi si presentarono con una raccomandazione scritta e firmata da tutti i membri del Gran Concilio — eccetto due che non si riuscì a scovare — perchè si dessero i denari richiesti.

Prima del meeting avevo ordinato di telegrafare a tutti gli "Up-State men" domandando il loro parere.

Risposero in favore del prelevamento.

Fui allora costretto a far votare. Non avevo più mezzi per impedirlo, dopo tre mesi di lotta.

Il prelevamento dal F. U. M. fu votato all'unanimità più uno, con entusiasmo e scoppio di applausi.

Come era possibile non firmare, in ossequio all'unanimità più uno, il check?

— Ma se per gli avvocati e pei delegati di Washington occorrevano quei danari, dove e come potevano raccoglierli?

— Avevo io stesso proposto mezzi legali e decenti, per esempio: domandare a tutte le Logge, padrone del Fondo, un'autorizzazione pel prelevamento. Ovvero chiedere alle Logge un prestito di 10 dollari o meno. Ma sempre a mezzo di un legale e legittimo consenso dei contributori, ossia dei padroni del danaro.

— Perchè le proposte non furono accetate?

— Per amore di cose facili e spicciative, e per quei tali metodi accennati, e che a me non garbano. Ora, devo dire che, per la verità e la buona regola, volli che tutto quanto avevo detto e fatto venisse registrato nei processi verbali.

— Sei sicuro che, in caso di contestazione, potrai riferirti a quei processi verbali e trovarli genuini?

— Oh! sì, non suppongo neppure che si arrivi a distruggere o falsificare dei documenti. Io posso riferirmi non solo ai Processi verbali, ma a documenti in mio possesso dai quali risulta come non solo mi opponevo all'illegalità, ma ne dicevo anche le ragioni, sperando fare intendere che il nero non è bianco.

— Or dunque si può dire che il fatto del prelevamento sia stata la sola ragione che ti fece abbandonare l'Ordine?

— No. Il prelevamento illegale fu la goccia che fa traboccare il vaso. Fu l'ultima di una serie di impressioni disgustose, prodotte dall'atmosfera dominante e dal retroscena. Un'atmosfera di odio individuale che opprime e disgusta. Io m'illudevo di poter attuare principii di progresso nell'interesse generale. Ero favorevole al proseguimento della causa, per stabilire nettamente i poteri nazionali ed i poteri statali. Ciò si poteva raggiungere senza perseguitare individui.

— Come?

— Si potevano stabilire i fatti d'accordo fra le parti, sui quali la Corte avrebbe deciso. Se l'accordo non poteva aver luogo, si poteva attenuare la lotta personale e concentrare la disputa intorno ai principi legali.

Le questioni da risolversi erano: 1. Il diritto o meno alla secessione. 2. La definizione precisa dei poteri della Suprema autorità. 3. I poteri dei Grandi Concilii e l'autonomia statale.

Ma che principi legali o costituzionali! Si trattava di vivacchiare alla meglio giorno per giorno, con spedienti e ripieghi. Si sosteneva per esempio, che il prelevamento si poteva fare, perchè **non si sarebbe saputo.**

Non si poteva discutere liberamente, perchè ogni argomento era considerato un'offesa personale ai prominenti, a pochi facendomi che monopolizzano l'Ordine, e sono dalla indifferenza della massa, abituati a non essere contradetti.

Si credeva che io avessi potuto sottomettermi a queste tradizioni dell'Ordine.

Mi ripugnava inoltre, l'ipocrisia predominante nei capi più influenti ed attivi.

Come mi scandalizzò l'uso non raro di brutalità non solo verbali, ma persino fisiche: maniche rimboccate, sbracciamenti, apostrofi provocanti, pugni chiusi, erano usuali.

Nella redazione dei processi verbali erano evidenti e sfacciate le omissioni e le lacune per indebolire gli argomenti degli oppositori.

Che meraviglia se quel comunicato ai giornali è falso, quando son falsi persino i processi verbali redatti, evidentemente, in **seguito ad** accordi?

Eccoti, anche, un piccolo esempio di misera fatuità.

Miele voleva essere qualche cosa nel Fondo Unico Mortuario, il fondo più grosso, e diviene, indovina che cosa: Presidente Onorario!

Si stampa la carta da lettere con questa intestazione: Grande Concilio Esecutivo con i nomi. Poi "Commissione Fondo Unico Mortuario" con a capo: "Presidente Onorario, Avv. Cav. Stefano Miele".

La cosa fece tale disgustosa impressione che molti protestarono, ed in nome della serietà della morte e del rispetto ai defunti, le lettere furono ristampate senza quel tragicomico Presidente Onorario.

In tale ambiente, qualunque tentativo per qualcosa di serio veniva soffocato.

L'angustia e la grettezza prevale anche nell'amministrazione. Chi lavora veramente per l'Ordine è pagato con salari di fame, ma si volevano prelevare $2500 per gli avvocati e $1700 pei delegati di Washington.

Miele diffondeva la notizia che lui comprò il mobilio per l'ufficio di Cleveland Place. In verità non fece che indurre il fratello ad indorsare una cambiale.

Io, presidente del F. U. M., non fui neppure consultato nella scelta degli impiegati, che vennero indicati e nominati da Miele.

Non ero sulle prime, che un Presidente decorativo, tanto vero che i Commissarii, nominati anche essi da Miele, si adunarono la prima volta ed apersero il meeting senza aspettare che giungesse il presidente.

Ciò mi consigliò di fare intendere loro, alla fine della seduta, che il nuovo Presidente non era una testa di legno, ma un uomo...

Ogni volta che si dovevano pagare $200 o 400 per un decesso, mi presentavano il check da firmare, ma non i documenti. Si usava così.

Le spese incontrate per gli emissari mandati in giro allo scopo di indurre le Logge a rimanere legate alla Convenzione di Schenectady o farvi aderire le neutrali, venivano caricate metà sul Fondo Unico Mortuario e metà sul Grande Concilio, senza autorizzazione nè della Commissione del Fondo, nè del Grande Concilio, il quale non andava pel sottile e ricevendo i Bills ne raccomandava il pagamento illegale al Fondo Unico Mortuario. Così furono pagati $60 a Pasquale Miele per aver visitato delle Logge.

Con queste esperienze mi recai alla Convenzione di Washington, per studiare se tali costumi erano locali nello Stato di New York, o generali in tutti gli Stati ove sono Logge di Figli d'Italia.

Constatai che l'influenza di Miele si estende dapertutto.

Non vidi allora possibilità nè di riforme nè di miglioramenti, a meno che un uomo intelligente ed energico dedicasse all'Ordine tutte le forze e tutto il tempo, ma, francamente non vale la pena.

La tribù dei Miele è in posizione strategica in tutto l'Ordine. Lo Avvocato Stefano, che domina lo Stato di New York, è nella Suprema. Un altro Miele è nel Gran Concilio; un terzo è nel Fondo Unico Mortuario.

Quel che accadde a Washington è noto: ventitrè delegati improvvisati; proroga con un colpo di mano dei poteri di Di Silvestro; trasferimento della sede del Supremo Concilio a Washington, per tenersi in contatto con politicanti americani a cui si magnifica la potenza di 300 mila Figli d'Italia, e con l'Ambasciatore non per assicurare vantaggi alla massa, ma onorificenze e prebende alla cricca dei caporioni.

Come me, tutti gli altri italo-americani devono ricusare di diventare strumenti e complici della "gang" che scoperti nei pochi mesi che feci parte dell'Ordine.

E credo ciò avverrà. Se l'Ordine non si modifica, liberandosi da coloro che lo sfruttano e lo abbassano, finirà per morire d'inedia. Che la mia esperienza valga per tutti gl'italiani seri e probi.

— Sicchè, quanto ti è costata la curiosità di ficcare il viso a fondo dell'Ordine dei Figli d'Italia?

— Non molto. Nove mesi di disgusto. Sei mesi di lavoro assiduo come avvocato della Grande Loggia e Presidente del F. U. M. ed oltre $500 di tasca.

Un'inezia di fronte al valore morale e sociale dell'insegnamento che da quanto scopersi e rivelai, possono trarre gl'italiani emigrati.

ERNESTO VALENTINI

COME SI ABUSA DELL'IGNORANZA
(Da Zarathustra di Aprile 1926)

Sempre a proposito dello sfacelo morale dell'Ordine

I riti, le leggi, i costumi ed il modo, come vive l'Ordine dei Figli d'Italia, presentano all'osservatore estraneo una delle forme caratteristiche con cui gli italiani più furbi sfruttano l'ignoranza e la dappocaggine dei lavoratori emigrati. Chi non conosce la cecità e la conseguente docilità dei connazionali?

Eccovi un esempio paradossale di come si trae profitto dalla superstizione e dall'ossessione del sovrumano e dell'ignoto, che opprime, molte volte, l'esistenza di uomini e donne del nostro popolo.

L'esempio del fattucchiero.

Sapete voi quanta povera gente crede, ancor'oggi, all'esistenza di fachiri cristiani, dotati di misteriose forze soprannaturali, per cui hanno potere di mutare le sorti d'un individuo, di liberarlo dalla miseria economica o da malattie inguaribili, o di propiziargli l'avvenire?

Lo sappiate, o non lo sappiate, facciamo un ipotesi, una semplice ipotesi.

Supponiamo un tipo astuto e perfido di avventuriero, che, mentre fra la classe elevata, passa per professionista, avvocato, computista, banchiere o altro, fra le donne del popolo si fa credere un Fattucchiero segreto, ma formidabile. Ha una moglie — supponiamo — che sa fingere, come Nino Pecoraro, di cadere in "trance!" ipnotica. Predice con essa il futuro. Indica la via della fortuna. Procura lavoro. Muta l'anima d'un marito infedele. Assicura l'amore del fidanzato tentennante, usando tutte le ciurmerie che si danno a credere ai poveri cretini.

Diamo un nome ipotetico a qualcuna delle vittime. Supponiamo che una, fra le tante, si chiami Malloni, e che questa, all'insaputa del marito, dapprima e poi col suo assenso, spogliandosi degli ultimi risparmi, impegnando i migliori oggetti della casa, porti tre o quattrocento dollari al mago, perchè gli "faccia la fattura" che dovrà redimerla dalla miseria ed addurre la ricchezza e la felicità nella famiglia.

Che direste voi, che direbbero gli americani fra cui viviamo, di questo mondo italiano? di siffatti individui che possono dedicarsi a tal genere di affari?

Ebbene, tutto ciò accade, si, accade fra noi, in questa America, qui dintorno, a New York, nel Jersey, accade più spesso di quel che si crede, accade in barba agli apostoli dell'educazione, alle Societies alle Welfare Leagues, ai giornali diffonditori enfatici di civiltà e... notizie false.

Assumereste voi il Fattucchiero a mentore, ispiratore e condottiero d'un Ordine come questo dei Figli d'Italia, i cui aderenti, per quattro quinti hanno l'angusta mentalità della nostra ipotetica Malloni, pronti a cadere nelle unghie rapaci dei Fattucchieri?

Ora, lo spirito che alita e tiene in vita l'Ordine dei Figli d'Italia, qual'esso è attualmente; lo spirito, che Roberto Ferrari scoperse e rivelò pel primo agli italiani, è uguale nell'essenza, nei fini, nella moralità e nelle ciurmerie, a quello del nostro ipotetico Fattucchiero.

APPENDICE
(Da Il Nuovo Vessillo, 7 Novembre 1925)

L'avv. Roberto Ferrari, presidente del Fondo Unico Mortuario della Grande Loggia di New York, ha scritto una lunga e dotta Monografia sulla crisi che dolorosamente travaglia l'Ordine "Figli d'Italia" in questo Stato. E la fa precedere da una prefazione con la quale mette in rilievo, in una forma limpida e sintetica, i fatti principali della vertenza e le ragioni giuridiche militanti in favore dell'Ordne. Questi fatti e queste ragioni. Egli enumera, sviluppa e semplifica nella Monografia che — scritta da un giurista profondamente edotto della questione come l'Avv. Ferrari, e ricca di argomenti sereni ed obbiettivi, costituisce un documento prezioso, indispensabile a tutti i Figli d'Italia che vogliono formarsi una coscienza più esatta, più precisa e più sicura sulle cause e sugli effetti del doloroso scisma che ha gravemente scosso la compagine numerica e spirituale della nostra Grande Loggia e della Comunità italiana in questo Stato.

"Il Nuovo Vessillo" che — libera e coraggiosa vedetta dei "Figli d'Italia" — è stato l'arma ideale della vittoriosa battaglia di Schenectady e che, dopo la infausta e nefasta secessione, ha intensificato, con maggior fede e vigore, la santa e generosa lotta contro i saccheggiatori del patrimonio sacro della nostra Grande Loggia, è oggi, lieto e orgoglioso del privilegio che gli accorda l'esimio Avv. Ferrari di pubblicare, cioè, la prefazione della splendida Monografia che, coi titoli di cui sopra, verrà prossimamente pubblicata, in edizione nitida ed elegante, e distribuita a beneficio del Fondo Unico Mortuario di Emergenza.

Con questa Monografia l'Avv. Roberto Ferrari prova a chiare note di voler tenere nobilmente fede alle promesse fatte nel suo primo comunicato alle Logge ed ai fratelli.

Con l'anima accesa dall'ardente passione per gl'ideali dell'Ordine, l'Avv. Ferrari dedica diuturnamente, da tre mesi, la sua prodigiosa intelligenza con la sua profonda coltura di giurista e la migliore parte della sua fenomenale attività al problema più assillante e più opprimente della nostra Grande Loggia, con la visione esatta e luminosa della bontà della accusa per cui combatte e della soluzione morale e giuridica della incresciosa e dolorosa vertenza culminata nell'illegale e delittuoso atta di secessione della "Sons of Italy Grand Lodge."

Della sua sorprendente attività e del suo magnifico e generoso contributo al dibattito ed al trionfo della causa dell'Ordine fanno fede i Memoriali, diligentemente e pazientemente preparati, gli articoli, i comunicati alla stampa e — non ultima — la Monografia in corso di stampa.

Senza posa e pretensione, l'Avv. Roberto Ferrari — figura nobile e diritta, integra ed austera — si va elevando sul piedistallo dell'ammirazione e della gratitudine dei "Figli d'Italia" non solo in questo Stato ma attraverso l'Unione.

LA DIREZIONE

Ecco la prefazione della interessante Monografia:

La scissura nella Grande Loggia dello Stato di New York dell'Ordine Figli d'Italia in America, che ebbe luogo il 6 Agosto 1925, mediante la secessione del gruppo appellante se stesso "Sons of Italy Grand Lodge" che tenne una Convenzione nella città di New York, ha causato grande confusione nella mente dei membri dell'Ordine e degli estranei all'Ordine circa le ragioni ed i torti nella questione.

Molti membri dell'Ordine mi hanno scritto o telefonato, per richiedermi informazioni sui fatti e le disposizioni di legge nonchè per la mia opinione al riguardo. Non è possibile rispondere a tutti individualmente.

Vi è molto in ciò che si dibatte e si discute che sa d'incerto e senza fondamento. Vi è la difficoltà di impostare le nostre argomentazioni sui fatti; e vi è inoltre la difficoltà di impostare le nostre argomentazioni sul disposto delle leggi. Vi è il lato legale della questione per stabilire quale sia la Grande Loggia legittima; se cioè la Gran Loggia che si riunì in Convenzione nella città di New York; ovvero la Grande Loggia che si riunì in Convenzione a Schenectady sotto gli auspicii della Suprema Loggia. Vi è inoltre coinvolta la questione morale per accertare quale Convenzione agì in accordo colle leggi, i costumi e le tradizioni dell'Ordine. Questa questione morale non può possibilmente essere decisa senza un'esame della storia dei fatti in questione. Il lato morale non può essere risoluto senza un'esame dei principii di legge e delle decisioni delle Corti.

Gli oratori a sostegno dell'una e dell'altra tesi vagano nell'incerto parlando delle varie Loggie subordinate, in questo critico momento quando ambo i lati desiderano il sostegno materiale e morale delle Loggie stesse, nel presentare i fatti nella complicata e controversa storia di questo caso e nella ricerca dei principii di legge e delle decisioni delle Corti da applicarsi nel caso presente. E' nostra lusinga che questa monografia possa risolvere le difficoltà incontrate dai suaccennati oratori.

L'opuscolo è specialmente dedicato ai fratelli dell'Ordine Figli d'Italia in America tanto nello Stato di New York che negli altri Stati della Unione. Per i membri dell'Ordine nello Stato di New York esso è di prima e vitale importanza, poichè sono essi che, in questo momento, debbono fare la grande decisione. Presentemente vi sono molti che si son rifugiati su terreno neutro, non sapendo a qual via appigliarsi. A questa grande massa di individui, desiderosi di conoscere alcuni degli elementi del caso, questo opuscolo, è sperabile possa riuscire di qualche utilità.

Mentre non vi è coinvolto un'immediato interesse finanziario per i membri dell'Ordine fuori dello Stato di New York, come vi è nel caso dei membri dell'Ordine nello Stato di New York, i membri dell'Ordine fuori dello Stato che hanno, a mezzo delle loro Grandi Loggie, espresso già la loro simpatia per la lotta del gruppo di Schenectady, sotto la protezione della Loggia Suprema, sono tuttavia vitalmente interessati dal punto di vista della solidarietà e della unità dell'Ordine negli Stati Uniti. Se la secessione può esser compiuta in uno Stato essa può essere compiuta negli altri Stati. Invece di avere un'Ordine unito, forte, potente attraverso gli Stati Uniti, noi avremo una serie di separate entità che avrebbero perduto il loro spirito, la loro importanza e la loro forza.

Io ho cercato di essere obbiettivo ed imparziale. Non so se vi sono riuscito. E' assai difficile, a dir poco, essere allo stesso tempo imparziale ed esatto specialmente quando si è coinvolti nella lotta. Ma ho fatto del mio meglio per presentare i fatti e le disposizioni di legge in una forma, per quanto possibile, accurata ed imparziale. Io non sono quindi sceso affatto a personalità. Nè mi son fermato a denunziare ed accusare. La questione che c'interessa è di principii e non di personalità. Non importa chi siamo gli individui. La storia è duratura e gli individui passano. Noi siamo interessati nel mantenere e stabilire un principio; e gli individui, se ve ne sono, che hanno violato i principii, non hanno alcun valore nel lungo e continuo flusso del tempo.

Infine, io ho cercato di presentare una serie di punti che potranno essere sviluppati dal lettore stesso, invece di una elaborata discussione degli stessi punti. Questo opuscolo si sarebbe potuto facilmente ampliare in modo da formare un libro. Ma chi avrebbe letto un libro? In questa epoca di frettoloso andare, anche gli uomini che han tempo a disposizione difficilmente leggono un libro di diverse centinaia di pagine. A me piace invece di stimolare l'intelligenza e l'abilità del lettore nello sviluppare i punti presentati dall'autore. Le amplificazioni, con un pò di buona volontà, possono facilmente farsi. In aggiunta, è da considerarsi il fatto che l'insieme dell'argomento può aversi più comprensivamente e completo quando il caso è presentato in una forma breve.

* * *

Il luogo stabilito dalla Convenzione della Grande Loggia dello Stato di New York, in Yonkers, nel 1924, per la Convenzione del 1925, fu Schenectady. Ciò era in accordo colle leggi ed i regolamenti dell'Ordine. Il giorno 20 Luglio, 1925, i membri dell'Ordine furono notificati che la Convenzione della Grande Loggia avrebbe avuto luogo in Schenectady secondo la deliberazione della ultima Convenzione della Grande Loggia. Il giorno 29 Luglio, 1925, il Grande Venerabile notificava i Delegati che la Convenzione non avrebbe avuto più luogo in Schenectady ma in New York. Un gruppo di Delegati e membri dell'Ordine obbiettò al trasferimento della sede della Convenzione a New York fece appello alla Suprema Loggia per avere una riunione della Gran Loggia dello Stato di New York, sotto gli auspici della Loggia Suprema, nel luogo designato dalla Convenzione del 1924. Ciò produsse uno stato di estrema confusione nelle fila della Grande Loggia dello Stato di New York. Alcuni Delegati si recarono alla Convenzione di New York ed altri Delegati andarono alla Convenzione di Schenectady.

I fondi dell'Ordine erano in possesso del gruppo che si riunì a New York; ed il macchinario amministrativo, perfezionato da molti anni di lavoro, era a loro disposizione. Il gruppo di Schenectady dovette creare un sistema di governo per l'amministrazione degli affari della Grande Loggia. Dovette stabilire un nuovo macchinario amministrativo, una nuova organizzazione ed escogitare mezzi immediati ed adatti per condurre a buon termine la nuova intrapresa. Fra i mezzi scelti per stabilire la nuova organizzazione vi fu quello del FONDO UNICO MORTUARIO DI EMERGENZA. Il Fondo Unico Mortuario dell'Ordine è una cosa che sta molto a cuore ai fratelli; ed era perciò naturale che il gruppo di Schenectady provvedesse i mezzi per collettare un fondo dal quale potessero essere pagati i benefici mortuari di modo che nessun beneficiario dei membri dell'Ordine avesse a soffrirne. Il piano prescelto fu il seguente:—

Le Loggie che non avevano pagato ancora il prospetto mensile, avrebbero pagato le quote di quel prospetto alla Grande Loggia per formare il nucleo del fondo di riserva; ed i membri delle Loggie subordinate, che erano rimaste fedeli all'Ordine, avrebbero fatto un prestito volontario di Un Dollaro a fratello. Questo fondo sarebbe stato usato per le spese amministrative al principio del difficile compito che si presentava alla Commissione del Fondo Unico Mortuario. Entro un mese dopo aver stabilita l'amministrazione del Fondo Unico Mortuario, DUE MILA DOLLARI FURONO PAGATI AI BENEFICIARI DI CINQUE FRATELLI MORTI, senza domandare ai membri che erano rimasti col gruppo di Schenectady di pagare qualsiasi quota come è stabilito dalla Costituzione e dalle Leggi dell'Ordine.

La divisione dello Stato di New York ha temporaneamente arrestato il movimento di consolidamento e di unificazione delle forze italiane negli Stati Uniti. Se questo modesto sforzo può riuscire utile in qualche maniera nel ravvivare ed invigorire l'Ordine nello Stato di New York, e nell'unificare l'Ordine in tutti gli Stati Uniti, l'autore e la Commissione del Fondo Unico Mortuario, per se, per l'Ordine ed in ispecial modo per il Fondo Unico Mortuario di Emergenza del gruppo di Schenectady, considereranno il loro lavoro e le loro cure ben spese.

ROBERTO FERRARI

LETTERA DELL'AVV. ROBERT FERRARI

alla stampa di New York

Chiarissimo Sig. Direttore del "Bollettino della Sera",

In risposta al Comunicato Ufficiale del Segretario del Fondo Unico Mortuario dell'Ordine Figli d'Italia Stato di New York, 27 Cleveland Place, la prego di pubblicare quanto segue:

Mi dimisi da Presidente della Commissione del Fondo Unico Mortuario, non per "ragioni mie personali" come si vuole far credere, ma per gravi ragioni d'ordine generale.

Non poteva accettare i metodi con cui si pretendeva io amministrassi il F. U. M.

Non potetti subire due prelevamenti di $2500.00 per gli avvocati della causa contro la Sons of Italy G. L. e $1700 per le spese dei delegati di Washington.

Ma quando l'unanimità dei Commissari insieme al Gran Concilio decisero per lo storno dei fondi, che per tre mesi avevo tentato di impedire, fui costretto, quale Presidente della Commissione, di firmare il check di $2500.00.

Un mio rifiuto ad apporre quella firma non sarebbe stato che un puerile tentativo di vano ostruzionismo.

Ma la firma del check non implica consenso o approvazione dell'atto illegale.

Ragioni più gravi e d'indole diversa contribuirono pure alla decisione di abbandonare l'Ordine.

Oltre al prelevamento illegale, che dimostra lo scarso ossequio dei dirigenti dell'Ordine verso le leggi, constatai;

1. Lo spirito tirannicamente predominante di pochi individui incapaci o indegni di dirigere una vasta organizzazione italiana, e la buona fede di quelli che supinamente si fanno travolgere ed ingannare.

2. Mezzi di azione subdoli, sleali ed ipocriti usati dai pochi dirigenti, come ne fanno prova anche il comunicato alla stampa con la falsa versione delle mie dimissioni.

3. Ostacolo tenace alla mia opera di Presidente del F. U. M.

4. Tendenza a sopraffarmi per vincere le mie — per essi — ubbie morali e legali.

5. Negligenza ed inaccortezza nella trattazione degli affari più delicati. Persino i verbali delle adunanze sono monchi e falsi.

6. Guerre, dissidi, denigrazioni dell'uno contro l'altro per interessi o ragioni unicamente personali.

7. Disinteresse ed indifferenza per ogni questione di vera e pratica utilità generale.

8. Disprezzo dei gregari, chiamati solo a contribuire pecuniariamente.

9. Mia irresistibile tendenza ad estrarmi dalle misere squisquiglie individuali per concentrare ogni sforzo su un programma di carattere sociale e culturale la cui attuazione mi era impedita.

10. Convinzione nata in me che questo sodalizio, come oggi, invece di promuovere e sviluppare la indispensabile fusione dell'elemento emigrato con quello indigeno e di conseguenza la prosperità e lo sviluppo degli italiani, non fa che ritardarlo, anzi impedirlo.

ROBERT FERRARI

QUEL CHE L'AVV. ROBERTO FERRARI RISPONDE AL COMUNICATO No. 2.

Seconda intervista con E. Valentini

S'intende che trattasi del comunicato del Grande Concilio dell'Ordine Figli d'Italia, dei figli cioè di Freschi e Di Silvestro.

Il comunicato No. 1, apparso nei quotidiani di New York, era di una trentina di righe, e pareva emanato dal Segretario del Fondo Unico Mortuario.

Fu oggetto d'un'intervista, così esauriente, da far credere chiusa con essa ogni disputa.

Invece no. Il 14 Aprile vien fuori, nel "Bollettino della Sera", il Comunicato No. 2, del Grande Concilio, un articolo lungo oltre 150 righe.

Nel giornale non ha firma. Ma in una circolare No. 21 "Ai Venerabili e Fratelli delle Logge dell'Ordine Figli d'Italia in America della Grande Loggia dello Stato di New York", in data 19 Aprile, vi si legge la firma di C. Pitocchi — Grande Segretario Archivista.

La questione era così riaperta. D'onde la necessità d'una seconda visita a Ferrari, per sentirne le impressioni e la versione Contraddittoria.

Bisogna però convenire che l'argomento, per se stesso antipatico, è diventato noioso e stantio, ma come fare, dappoichè si è in ballo?

Eccomi, dunque, nuovamente dall'avvocato Ferrari.

— Ah, sì? — gli dissi — tu usi "con tanta leggerezza la parola falso ed hai persino resi "dolenti" i Figli. Spiegati, spiegati subito. Era falso il Comunicato, o sei leggero tu? Quanto pesi, settantacinque libbre?

— Non scherzare, o non ti rispondo. E' possibile che tu non possa parlare, o sentir parlare dell'Ordine Figli d'Italia, senza metterti di buon umore? Stammi dunque a sentire e risponderò a questo comunicato, tanto lungo quanto vuoto, punto per punto.

Dissi che il primo comunicato era falso, perchè parlava di ragioni personali e particolari, che non esistevano, e taceva intorno ai guai impersonali, riguardanti l'Ordine, che non esposi nella lettera di dimissione — è vero —, ma comunicai verbalmente a tre ufficiali del Grande Concilio, compreso il Grande Venerabile, nonchè al Comitato di 15 Grandi Delegati, che venne a richiedermi di ritirare le dimissioni.

A questo Comitato parlai, nel mio ufficio, quattro ore, dalle 5 alle 9 p. m. Nella lettera non erano le motivazioni in dieci parole, ma esse furono partecipate ai Grandi delegati, quella sera, in un volume.... parlato.

Vuoi poi sapere perchè omisi le ragioni nella lettera? perchè avrebbero contenuto una critica amara, che per un senso di delicatezza intendevo tenere nel fondo dell'anima senza esporla al pubblico.

Fu il loro comunicato che annullò la necessità d'ogni riserbo, d'un riserbo mantenuto da ma per due mesi.

Essi, infatti, parlarono di ragioni particolari, non precisando nessuna di queste ragioni, facendo correre la fantasia del pubblico chi sa dove; essi allusero alla firma del check, omettendo le mie ostinate obbiezioni alla creazione di quel check, facendo credere che avessi approvato la prelevazione del Fondo Mortuario, per questo dovetti dire e dissi le vere ragioni tanto a te, quanto nella risposta ai giornali.

Così, non è vero che io abbia assicurato i Delegati che non avrei "mai permesso agli avversari di speculare sulle mie dimissioni ai danni dell'Ordine". Io, che non ignoro le complicazioni e le sorprese della vita, non avrei mai fatta una promessa incondizionata di quel genere. Mi sarei legato, perchè "promissio boni viri est obligatio" e quando fossi stato attaccato mi sarei trovato nella impossibilità di rispondere.

Dissi chiaramente al Comitato dei Grandi Delegati, durante il lungo discorso, cui ho accennato, che non prometteva di non parlare e tutto sarebbe dipeso dalle circostanze e dall'avvenire.

Aggiungo ora, che, se anche avessi promesso — ciò che escludo — il comunicato mendace mandato alla stampa e senza consultarmi, mi avrebbe liberato da ogni promessa.

— Adesso intendo perchè quando ti interrogai insistentemente dopo la Convenzione di Washington non volesti dir nulla. Ora senti:

Qui è scritto "Più tardi l'Avv. Ferrari, che aveva rifiutato di ricevere il Comitato del Grande Concilio, accettava invece di ricevere, non sappiamo con quanta proprietà, un Comitato di Grandi Delegati, i quali insistevano per il ritiro delle sue dimissioni".

Puoi spiegarmi, innanzi tutto, questo importante inciso "non sappiamo con quanta proprietà?" vuol dire forse che ricevere il Comitato del G. Concilio era proprio, ma era improprio ricevere i Grandi Delegati? Non sono tutti Figli... legittimi ed ugualmente grandi?

— Non scherzare. Senti quel che ti dico. Ero entrato nell'Ordine con entusiasmo e fede. La disillusione mi sfiancò. Non si lavora sei mesi assiduamente per l'Ordine, e la sua causa, non si lavora di giorno e di notte senza la fede in un ideale. Sognavo fare dei Figli d'Italia una forza sociale, di spingerli nella vita americana, di conseguire risultati pratici visibili. Invece nulla era possibile. Il disgusto mi vinse al punto che sulle prime non volevo sentire più nemmeno parlare dell'Ordine. Così fu che rifiutai ricevere il Comitato del Grande Concilio ed eccoti copia della lettera mia, da cui traspare il mio stato d'animo. Dice:

February 15, 1926.

Mr. Francis J. Panetta, Order Sons of Italy,
27 Cleveland Place, — New York City.

Dear Frank:

I have received your message telling me that a committee of the Grand Council would like to wait upon me.

I have the utmost respect for the committee of the Grand Council but no useful purpose can be served by my meeting them. I dislike to rake over dying members.

Let them die.

My decision is irrevocable.

I have also resigned from the Order Sons of Italy in America.

With kindest personal regards, I am, cordially yours

ROBERT FERRARI

— Sta bene. Vieni ora all'"improprietà".

— Dopo alcune settimane, le prime impressioni si attutirono. Potevo considerare le cose e parlarne senza appassionarmi, accettai quindi — poichè insistevano — di ricevere il Comitato dei Grandi Delegati, ma per non aver l'aria di ignorare il Grande Concilio, invitai anche due membri di esso. Uno fu presente, e l'altro non venne, benchè avessi telefonato due volte al suo ufficio alla presenza dei Delegati.

— Spiega ora che cosa è l'affare del revolver che, secondo un giornale, sarebbe stato usato per farti firmare il check.

— E la prima volta che ne sento parlare.

Io, che pur leggo molti giornali, non vidi nulla di simile. Sai il nome del giornale?

— Assolutamente no.

— E' strano che il Comunicato non citi quel giornale responsabile d'una così grave notizia.

— L'avranno dimenticato. Ma via, se fosse vera la storiella del giornale X perchè non domandare a me immediatamente una smentità, piuttosto che venir fuori col comunicato falso e subdolo delle "ragioni particolari"?

E' curioso essere accusato, come nel comunicato, di mancare di elementare senso di giustizia su cosa assolutamente ignorata da me, e forse, chi sa?, persino inesistente. Se almeno mi avessero avvertito della tragicomica storiella del check col revolver alla gola, il senso di giustizia — come dicevo — si sarebbe svegliato in me, te lo assicuro.

— Più oltre è detto "Egli preferì mantenersi in un compiacente silenzio". Che vuol dire "compiacente silenzio?" Chi volevi compiacere? chi ti aveva puntato il revolver, o il giornale che ti faceva passare per la docile vittima d'un Hold Up?

— No. Secondo il comunicato, io sarei diventato d'un tratto partigiano dei Sons of Italy, e poichè la storiella dell'Hold Up — come tu dici — poteva gettare un'ombra livida contro quelli di Schenectady, io avrei lasciato correre la notizia, senza smentirla.

Dirai che tutto questo è stupido, è bambinesco. Ebbene sono così: quando fanno gli uomini pubblici che declamano e scrivono pei giornali, arrivano sin dove sono arrivati coi comunicati; quando sono i tecnici dell'Ordine, e ne maneggiano i danari, fanno come quando me **ne dovetti andare.**

I metodi dei caporioni — non dell'Ordine in massa, bada bene — son questi e non si smentiscono mai, tanto sono connaturati e sangue del loro sangue.

— Che puoi dire del Grande Concilio, che indisse il Grande Comizio del 28 Marzo? Come potettero "dichiarare — a quanto dicono nel Comunicato — che le dimissioni dell'Avvocato Ferrari erano un fatto suo personale, e ciò in base alle sue non motivate dimissioni"? Se non erano motivate, come risultarono a loro i motivi personali?

— Il fatto sta che sapevano perfettamente le vere ragioni e sapevano pure che non erano personali.

— Un'altra cosa: le dichiarazioni da te fatte nel tuo Comunicato alla stampa sono dallo stesso Grande Concilio qualificate di "una gravità impressionante se rispondenti a "verità".

L'unica cosa da essi prodotta per distruggerle è la nuda, secca, sgusciante affermazione che non rispondono a verità.

Ma, poichè quelle ragioni, giudicate così gravi, vennero da te illustrate e dettagliate nel "Nuovo Mondo" con nomi e citazioni di parole precise, com'è che nel comunicato ultimo non se ne parla neppure? Sta a vedere che non lessero la nostra intervista. Mandagliene almeno una copia, ogni due grandi Ufficiali; non essere avaro.

— Caro Valentini, quando certe posizioni non si possono superare, si girano prudentemente, fingendo di non vederle. Tu supponi che non abbiano letto il "Nuovo Mondo?" Io suppongo invece che dopo averlo letto tre volte, abbiano deciso di non averlo letto.

— Che puoi dire intorno ai prelevamenti?

— La cosa è semplice e chiara. La proposta fu per due prelevamenti: $2500 per gli avvocati, $1700 pei delegati. Mi opposi ad entrambi perchè abusivi ed illegali.

Dopo due mesi di lotta e di resistenza da parte mia si consultarono gli avvocati americani, che si pronunziarono per la illegalità dei $1700 pei delegati. Si prelevarono allora i $2500 per gli avvocati.

Non è vero io abbia dato ad intendere di aver dovuto resistere a due prelevamenti. Il mio statement ai giornali disse così:

"Non potetti subire due prelevamenti di $2500 per gli avvocati della causa contro i Sons of Italy G. L. e $1700 per le spese dei delegati di Washington.

"Ma quando l'unanimità dei Commissari, insieme al Gran Concilio, decise per lo storno dei fondi, che per tre mesi avevo tentato di impedire, fui costretto, quale Presidente della Commissione, di firmare il check di $2,500".

— Che puoi dire dei processi verbali da te giudicati monchi e falsi e che poi firmasti? Leggi quel che scrivono: "L'Avv. Ferrari parla di processi verbali monchi e falsi, ma tutti i processi verbali portano la sua firma e se egli li avesse riscontrati monchi e falsi avrebbe dovuto avere la bontà ed il coraggio di non firmarli".

— Dico che questa è una flagrante bugia.

Non è vero che io abbia firmato nessuno dei processi verbali delle discussioni intorno al prelevamento dei $2500. Infatti i processi verbali, dal 14 dicembre 1925 al 3 febbraio 1926, quando mi dimisi, non furono firmati da me.

— Perchè non li firmasti?

— Perchè essendo monchi e falsi, non volli riconoscerli.

— Non avevi modo di ottenere verbali genuini e veritieri?

— No, perchè le pressioni sul segretario erano più forti della sua resistenza. Colui che aveva presentato alla Commissione del F. U. M. le proposte di storno, proposte che io avevo tacciate di irregolarità, non voleva che l'opera sua risultasse dai processi verbali. Ti dò un esempio.

— Un esempio? Ricordi forse i processi verbali a memoria?

— No, sapendo l'umore delle mie bestie, me ne feci fare una copia, che ritengo a mia difesa.

Il processo verbale del 14 dicembre 1925 dice così: "Pro Litem. "Dopo lunghe ed importanti discussioni alle quali prendono parte il Presidente, ecc. ecc., intorno ad un prestito di $2500 da farsi dall'Amministrazione del Fondo Unico Mortuario, per la lite pendente innanzi alle Corti, si conviene di aggiornare questa parte dell'Ordine del Giorno ad altra seduta da destinarsi".

Letto il verbale, nella copia mandatami un mese dopo dal segretario, scrissi una lettera, facendo notare che nel verbale era stato omesso l'autore della proposta, ed erano state soppresse le obbiezioni da me fatte contro di essa, non che le ragioni che avevo presentate davanti la Commissione, tacendo, persino, la mia opposizione generica.

Nella lettera notai, che intorno alla questione più grave aveano soppresso la posizione da me presa.

Che te ne pare? Vuoi un altro esempio di come erano redatti i verbali?

Lo stesso individuo autore delle due proposte di storno, suggerì che, come di consueto, si prelevassero $200 per l'Ospedale Italiano. Il processo verbale dice invece: "Il presidente fa vive raccomandazioni perchè l'Amministrazione, seguendo l'esempio del Grande Concilio voglia concorrere con la spesa di $200 pel mantenimento dell'ospedale italiano"

Perchè sostituire il vero proponente col proponente che non avea detto verbo?

Ebbene, tali inesattezze e lacune, non sono casuali, furono però rilevate nella lettera cui ho accennato.

Infine, per dimostrare come il mio stato d'animo erasi venuto gradatamente formando, e da lungo tempo, ecco quello che, alla vigilia della partenza per Washington, dissi al Grande Venerabile in questa lettera che puoi pubblicare. Bada che la lettera tendeva anche a sbugiardare coloro che mi accusavano di tirannia e prepotenza, perchè non mi decidevo a mettere ai voti la proposta del prelevamento dei $2500.

January 28, 1926.

Honorable John Freschi,

50 Pine Street,

New York City.

Dear John:

I have been reliably informed that it is the general opinion among people of our group of the Order Sons of Italy, that in declining to grant a loan from the Mortuary Fund in order to pay attorneys with, and to grant another loan of $1700, for the payment of the expenses of the Supreme delegates to Washington. I have been acting in an autocratic manner and as an anemy of the Order.

This is simply outrageous. If anybody should complain of autocracy, it is I. I have given other people full liberty to express their ideas and I have taken that right myself. Others, however, have attempted to gain their ends by moral coercion and physical compulsion. If we have not seen eye to eye it is unfortunate, but certainly such extravagent charges are idiotic.

I do not desire to obstruct your proceedings in any manner. I ame therefore willing, indeed eager at the present moment and before the Convention meets to hand in my resignation to take effect im**mediately.**

I shall give my reasons to an impartial world and let that world judge between my opponents and me.

Cordially yours,

ROBERT FERRARI

Caro Valentini, mi accusano di essere metafisico. Accetto l'accusa, e mi compiaccio con me stesso.

Affermano, a lor volta, di essere pratici e di conoscere le vie che menano, nella vita, a sicuri successi.

Non li contraddico. Però è questione di gusti. Sono avvocato penale e per esperienza professionale conosco quelle vie. Qualche volta, molte volte, riescono. Ma tal'altra no; perchè, sai? sono le vie di Gerald Chapman.